Prentice Hall Series in
Advanced Business Communication

Guide to
Business Etiquette

Roy Cook
Gwen Cook
Laura Yale
Fort Lewis College

Mary Munter
Series Editor
Tuck School at Dartmouth College

PEARSON

Prentice
Hall

Upper Saddle River, New Jersey 07458

Library of Congress Cataloging-in-Publication Data

Cook, Roy A.

Guide to business etiquette / Roy Cook, Gwen Cook, Laura Yale.

p. cm. — (The Prentice Hall series in advanced communication)

ISBN 0-13-144917-6

1. Business etiquette I. Cook, Gwen. II. Yale, Laura J. III. Title. IV. Series.

HF5389.C655 2005

395.5'2—dc22   2004006365

Senior Editor: David Parker
Editorial Director: Jeff Shelstad
Project Manager: Ashley Keim
Assistant Editor: Melissa Yu
AVP/Exec. Marketing Manager: Shannon Moore
Marketing Assistant: Patrick Danzuso
Senior Managing Editor (Production): Judy Leale
Production Editor: Theresa Festa

Associate Director, Manufacturing: Vincent Scelta
Production Manager: Arnold Vila
Manufacturing Buyer: Michelle Klein
Cover Design: Kiwi Designs
Cover Illustration/Photo: Kiwi Designs
Composition/Full-Service Project Management: Carlisle Communications
Printer/Binder: Phoenix Book Tech/Phoenix

Credits and acknowledgments borrowed from other sources and reproduced, with permission, in this textbook appear on appropriate page within text.

Pearson Education LTD.
Pearson Education Singapore, Pte. Ltd.
Pearson Education, Canada, Ltd.
Pearson Education—Japan

Pearson Education Australia PTY, Limited
Pearson Education North Asia Ltd
Pearson Educación de Mexico, S.A. de C.V.
Pearson Education Malaysia, Pte. Ltd

10 9 8 7 6 5 4
ISBN 0-13-144917-6

Contents

CHAPTER 4

COMMUNICATION ETIQUETTE   41

CHAPTER 5

BASIC BUSINESS DINING ETIQUETTE   57

CHAPTER 6

SPECIAL DINING EVENTS   71

Introduction

HOW THIS BOOK CAN HELP YOU

This book is for you if you want to secure a foundation of business etiquette knowledge, to answer specific etiquette questions, and to put your best foot forward to be recognized as a professional. The book will answer questions such as:

- How do I introduce others and myself?
- How do I dress for different occasions?
- What is the etiquette for a job interview?
- How can I handle conflict in the office?
- How can I take stress out of business travel?
- What is the etiquette for telephone, email, and other kinds of communication?
- How can I be an effective host or guest during business meals?
- How do I moderate a meeting?
- How do etiquette rules change in international settings?

If you want to learn about business etiquette in general, read through this entire book. If you already know the basics of business etiquette, skim for specific, straightforward answers to your questions. You will then be able to:

- Double check your knowledge to avoid potential etiquette blunders.
- Learn more and refine your skills.
- Become familiar with a quick reference resource for answers on how to deal with new situations or provide answers to recurring etiquette questions.

Perhaps most importantly, this book will help you appear poised, confident, and professional by providing essential information and practical examples of important etiquette practices in today's changing working environment.

WHO CAN USE THIS BOOK

This book was written for you if you want to become more adept at business etiquette—those important do's and don'ts for every business setting. Here are just a few reasons why mastering the basics of business etiquette is so important to your career.

- Etiquette mistakes can result in lost jobs, lost sales, and poor working relationships.
- You spend the majority of your working hours interacting with people. Learning the etiquette necessary to navigate these working relationships successfully gives you confidence and poise.
- Those who practice business etiquette are respected and recognized for their professionalism.
- Maneuvering successfully in cross-cultural situations can save you career-embarrassing *faux pas*.
- Basic business etiquette is expected, but rarely taught.

WHY THIS BOOK WAS WRITTEN

We have conducted seminars and coached students as well as experienced managers on the basics of business etiquette for years. After many discussions, it became clear to us that, no matter who was asking the questions about proper etiquette, those questions began to show similarities: it seems business people have many of the same concerns and discomforts when it comes to questions of etiquette.

As we searched for a book that provided clear, concise, and useful guidelines for these questions, we were disappointed. What we found tended to fall into one of two categories: one group of books was both cutesy and almost flippant about etiquette issues; the second group read like tomes covering everything you could ever think to ask—and in excruciating detail.

To fill that gap and address the needs of busy professionals, Prentice Hall has created the Prentice Hall Series in Advanced Business Communication: brief, practical, reader-friendly guides for people who communicate in professional contexts. (See the inside front cover for more information on the series.) Like the other books in the series, this book is . . .

- *Brief:* The book summarizes key ideas only. Culling from thousands of pages of text, we have omitted bulky examples, cases, footnotes, exercises, and discussion questions

- *Practical:* This book offers clear, straightforward tools you can use. It includes only information you will find useful in a professional context.

- *Reader-friendly:* We have tried to provide an easy-to-skim format using a direct, matter-of-fact, nontheoretical tone. Those hoping to gain new ideas can read it in its entirely; those wishing to refresh their memory should be able to skim specific pages easily.

HOW THIS BOOK IS ORGANIZED

For ease of use and reference, we have divided this book into eight, self-contained chapters. Each chapter is packed with useful information for everyday and special business settings and occasions.

Chapter 1: Understanding the Rules of Etiquette

A quick trip back through history sets the stage for etiquette practices today. Although some things have changed, many modern rules of engagement are deeply rooted in the practices of the past. The chapter concludes by exploring what you need to know to work confidently in today's changing business world.

Chapter 2: Creating a Powerful First Impression

Learn to make the most out of the powerful messages you send by how you dress, make introductions, shake hands, and carry on conversations during first encounters. In addition, this chapter pays special attention to interviewing skills, one of the most difficult relationship-building situations we face during our careers.

Chapter 3: Maintaining Business Relationships

Maintaining positive and productive working relationships requires effort on your part. Learn how to deal effectively with the inevitable conflict that finds its way into working relationships. Discover how to destress travel, deal with your own or others' romantic inclinations, and how to maneuver effectively through your physical working environment.

Chapter 4: Communication Etiquette

This chapter provides an overview of communication etiquette—written and oral—to use in the wide variety of channels we use today (ranging from email to telephone to face-to-face). Learn how to identify your audience, then construct and deliver effective messages.

Chapter 5: Basic Business Dining Etiquette

Business dining is much more than sitting down to a meal. This chapter equips you with the fundamental etiquette basics for typical dining settings, from breakfast through dinner. Learn what is expected of you as a host or a guest.

Chapter 6: Special Dining Events

Special dining events can be a bit intimidating by their very nature: they are special! We take the mystery and possible intimidation out of formal events by deconstructing the courses at a meal and setting and walking through the basic do's and don'ts. You will also learn how to enjoy yourself at banquets, celebrations, and casual business dining settings.

Chapter 7: Successful Meetings

This chapter covers what to do before, during, and after a meeting. Learn how to be a productive organizer, facilitator, and participant.

Chapter 8: Cross-Cultural Etiquette

Venturing into the international business arena requires learning a new set of etiquette skills. In this chapter, you will learn the nuances needed to greet people and build relationships in various cultures. Eye-opening examples will alert you to the importance of studying other cultures in detail if you want to avoid embarrassing cultural *faux pas*.

BIBLIOGRAPHY

Throughout the book, we provide practical advice for novices just entering the work world, as well as for seasoned executives seeking to keep their business etiquette skills on the cutting edge. In the bibliography at the end of the book, we include a list of references for those interested in exploring a subject in more depth.

ACKNOWLEDGMENTS

We are grateful for the broad-based help and support we received while developing this project. Successful completion would not have been possible without the encouragement of friends, colleagues, and family members. Special thanks to Kay Baker, Cameron Clarkson, Skip Cave, Rose Clay, Larry Goff, Tracey Imel, Jan Scott, Carol Stoner, Allyn Talg, Chuck Tustin, and Chuck Yoos. Particular appreciation is extended to Professor Mary Munter, our series editor: her skills, patience, creativity, guidance, and depth of knowledge were a source of inspiration. Finally, thanks go to our parents for bringing us up right and teaching us that "manners matter." There is nothing like a good foundation from which to grow.

Roy Cook
Gwen Cook
Laura Yale
Fort Lewis College

Guide to
Business Etiquette

CHAPTER I OUTLINE

1. Etiquette lessons from history
   The ideals of chivalry
   The fork
   Chopsticks
   Sixteenth-century table manners
   Seventeenth-century table manners
   Round-ended knives
   Nineteenth-century table manners
   Twentieth-century table manners
   Current practices rooted in history

2. The basis of etiquette today
   Remember the little things
   Be civil
   Follow the "Golden Rule"
   Don't try to be perfect
   Change with the times
   Beware of the generation gap
   Be ethical

CHAPTER 1

Understanding the Rules of Etiquette

Who came up with the ideas that you should keep your elbows off the table or that you should extend your hand to shake when meeting someone? Are the customs of old still appropriate today? Who decided what constitutes good manners? How and where were these standards for good manners determined? How do we decide what social behaviors and actions are right and wrong in today's business settings? Finding the answers to these and many more questions may mean flipping back through the pages of history to explore the worldwide origins of today's etiquette.

Although it wasn't always called "etiquette," the practice of manners is as old as the human race. Even before recorded history, there is evidence of good manners for the times. We wouldn't consider the early cave dwellers well mannered, but they had manners that were appropriate for their time. They quickly learned that, to get along with each other, they had to share and work together. This ability to get along with one another has been called many things over the years—civility, good manners, comportment, decorum, courtesy, politeness, respect, and deportment to name a few. Regardless of what these rules of engagement and the understood codes of conduct are called, one thing is certain: they add a degree of certainty to how we interact with each other. Knowing basic business etiquette is not a luxury. It is a necessity for career advancement.

1. Etiquette lessons from history

Formal etiquette, or accepted rules of conduct, began to appear long ago. Even though many of those accepted practices are centuries old, they still provide guidance for our actions today.

The ideals of chivalry: When feudalism reached its highest pinnacle in the twelfth and thirteenth centuries, chivalry was the ideal of courteous knightly conduct, stressing loyalty and obeisance by a knight to his God, his lord, and his lady. Originating in France and Spain, chivalry soon spread throughout the Continent and to England. It was a fusion of Christian and military ideals with piety, loyalty, bravery, and honor as virtues.

- *Chivalric seating arrangements:* At meals, people always waited for those of higher rank to be served. This is where the phrase "seated above the salt" originated. Salt was a very expensive commodity at this time, and only those of high rank and fortune could afford it. To be seated above the salt meant that you were seated where you could use the salt provided by your host.

- *Chivalric plate sharing:* The knight and his lady shared a "trencher," that is, a stale piece of bread that was used as a plate during the meal. He used his knife to cut a large portion of meat to be placed on the trencher, and then cut the meat into smaller pieces for consumption. The knight always made sure that his lady received the choicest piece of meat from the trencher. He also used his knife to spear any vegetables that might accompany the meal. Once the meal was finished, the trenchers, which by then were softened by the absorbed juices from the meal, were eaten by the servants.

The fork: The story of how the fork made its way to the table is a tale of romance and a journey across continents and civilizations. It began sometime around the year 1000 when a nobleman from Venice was traveling through the Middle East. He met a beautiful Turkish princess and fell in love. After a very brief courtship, they were married and returned to Venice. In her dowry was a box of eating utensils common to the Middle East since around 600 but oddities in Venice. These strange utensils were forks.

Needless to say, a foreign princess who practiced this strange way of eating with a fork instead of a knife and fingers caused quite a stir.

However, as sensible as it may seem today, the fork's place at the table was short lived. Church leaders were appalled at the use of this utensil. After all, they said, it was an insult to God who had given people fingers for eating. When the princess became ill and died, they felt vindicated and said that her death was caused by the use of the fork. Thus, the fork fell into disfavor and became an object to be avoided.

This strange pronged eating utensil did not reappear on the tables of Italians for over 300 years. But it was the Italians, specifically Catherine de Médici of Florence, who introduced it to the rest of Europe. In 1533, she brought several of these unique eating instruments with her as she moved to Paris after her marriage to King Henry II. By the mid-1600s, the practice of dipping one's hands into a common eating pot was no longer acceptable.

Chopsticks: Long before the fork began to be used in the Middle East, another eating utensil—chopsticks—was finding its way into common usage in China. Rather than sticking a knife into a common pot, the Chinese used chopsticks to fish out their food. The story of chopsticks is almost as interesting as that of the fork, although perhaps it is not as romantic.

The practice of the time was to cook food in a pot that hung from a tripod over an open fire. When the food was cooked, the pot would be set aside to cool. After a sufficient cooling period, it was then safe to reach in and grab a piece of whatever had been cooking. One ingenious and hungry diner figured out that, if you used two sticks to reach into the boiling pot, you could be first and get the choicest and biggest piece of meat. This trick caught on fast and everyone wanted a pair of chopsticks. Why wait for the pot to cool?

Some people believe that Confucius, a vegetarian, influenced the adoption of chopsticks. He thought that knives represented violence, and therefore should not be used at the table. During the Middle Ages, the nobility preferred silver chopsticks because they believed silver changed colors once it came in contact with poison.

Sixteenth-century table manners: Another important event for etiquette came in 1530, when Erasmus, a Dutch humanist, wrote *On Civility in Children*. This work was translated into English in 1532 and quickly became a standard for proper behavior. Because his book was translated into many languages and reprinted numerous times, his easy-to-follow admonishments for acceptable behavior were adopted and followed by the upper class in England and all across Europe.

Erasmus introduced the idea and importance of practicing table manners. His rules of proper conduct may seem quite crude today, but they were revolutionary at the time. If you think gathering at the table for a meal is sometimes a little chaotic today, imagine sitting down to a meal in Erasmus' time, when everyone dined from a common pot, seated crammed around a table, and reached into the pot to grab their shares of the meal. This was the setting and customs of the time when he introduced the following rules for proper table manners. They may seem crude by today's standards, but were very practical for the time.

- Cut and clean your fingernails before dining.
- Don't pick your nose while eating.
- Don't throw bones you have chewed on back into the pot. Lay them on the table or throw them on the floor.
- Use only three fingers to reach into the pot, not your whole hand.
- Take the first piece of meat you touch.
- Don't clean your teeth with your knife.
- Don't lick greasy fingers or wipe them on your coat; use the tablecloth instead.

Seventeenth-century table manners: During this century, a new word entered the vocabulary of the day: "etiquette." This French word soon found a permanent home in our everyday vocabulary though common usage. Take a look at almost any dictionary and you will find a definition similar to this: "the forms, manners, and practices dictated by social custom or authority." But how did this word come to be used?

The use of the actual word "etiquette" seems to have first appeared in the 1600s, when lists of rules and regulations called *l'estiquette* were posted by the nobility to provide guidance on proper behavior for those entering palace grounds on ceremonial occasions, especially to dine. The idea of this list came from documents that were attached to the outside of packages to indicate their contents. These lists evolved into printed rules of specific do's and don'ts that protected people from doing anything that might appear foolish in the presence of royalty. King Louis XIV of France brought this practice to its zenith during his seventy-two-year reign. Of course, society of that time was different from that of today. It was a time when the king or queen could say "Off with their heads"— and literally mean it. Anyone who wanted to stay in the good graces of their sovereigns obeyed the rules of the day. Those rules included statements that may seem odd today.

- Eat only with your thumb, index, and middle finger (not the whole hand, which was common practice at the time).

- If you are not using your knife to eat, keep it in its sheath. (There is no need to appear threatening to those around you.)

- Keep your elbows off the table (thus providing more room for others at a typically crowded table, where two people shared one plate and everyone at the table shared the same drinking vessel).

- Don't pick your teeth with your knife while sitting at the table (that was just disgusting and unsightly).

The edicts of royalty even affected table utensils.

Round-ended knives: You use them every day and probably even take the design of table knives for granted. Yet, in medieval times, when people ate from a common pot, knives needed to be pointed to stab and retrieve food from the common pot. Therefore, with the introduction of the fork, pointed knives were no longer necessary. But why did the points disappear?

There are two stories about the design we see today. One says that Cardinal Richelieu of France was disgusted by one of his guests, who continually picked his teeth with his knife while seated at the table. To cure this problem, the cardinal ordered that the points be ground off all the table knives. The other story is also a practical one. In 1669, King Louis XIV of France issued a decree making it illegal to carry, make, or set tables with pointed knives. In an effort to prevent violence, he also ordered that the points of all knives be ground off, leaving them rounded. Whichever story is true, the effect was the same: the practice spread rapidly throughout Europe and the pointed table knife became an artifact of history.

Nineteenth-century table manners: During the late 1800s, books on etiquette appeared in a steady succession. Rules regarding proper behavior for meals were very specific and included advice such as:

- Don't tuck your napkin under your chin or spread it upon your breast; bibs and tuckers are for the nursery. Don't spread your napkin over your lap; let it fall over your knee.
- Don't eat from the end of your spoon; eat from the side.
- Don't gurgle, draw in your breath, or make other noises when eating soup. Don't ask for a second service of soup.
- Don't eat vegetables with a spoon; eat them with a fork. The rule is not to eat anything with a spoon that can be eaten with a fork. Even ices were to be eaten with a fork.
- Don't leave your knife and fork on your plate when you send it for a second supply.

Twentieth-century table manners: With the affluence and free time created by the Industrial Revolution, the attention of the rising middle class turned to social niceties rather than day-to-day survival. The aspiring middle class now wanted to emulate the proper manners in which the upper classes had been schooled since birth. To meet this need, a wide variety of etiquette books offering rules for proper behavior in almost every situation began to appear.

Emily Post (1872–1960) probably shaped today's etiquette landscape in our society more than any other person did. She was so important to the development of modern etiquette that she became known as the authority on social behavior, giving rise to the acceptance of etiquette by the middle class. Her unique gift of bringing the grace of etiquette into everyday life by removing the aura of snobbery and stiffness encouraged everyone to practice good manners. Her first book, *Etiquette: The Blue Book of Social Usage* (1922), provided practical etiquette advice that anyone could use.

Current practices rooted in history: Many of our actions and items that we unconsciously accept as standards of behavior or usage are rooted in practicality. Take, for example, dinner conversation, shaking hands, offering a toast, and using a fork. All have found their way into the twenty-first century, following long and time-honored traditions.

- *Dinner conversation:* When food was no longer devoured simply for survival, eating became a social activity. Freed from the fear of starvation, the Egyptians, Greeks, and Romans considered it polite to visit and even enjoy a little entertainment before, during, and after dining. It soon became an accepted belief that enjoyable conversation helped with the digestion of the meal and that food was meant to be enjoyed.

- *Shaking hands:* The practice of extending and shaking the right hand when greeting one another dates back to medieval times. In those days, men carried knives that functioned both as an eating utensil and as a weapon. Because anyone you met could be a threat, it became a common practice to extend your open hand as a nonthreatening gesture of greeting, showing that you came in peace.

- *The toast:* Another example of extending a symbol of nonviolence can be seen in the symbolism of the toast. In offering a toast, the chalices were "clinked" together vigorously so that the contents of one chalice would slosh into the other. This simple gesture showed that the person proposing the toast had not poisoned the drink, and it was safe for both parties to drink. Raising cups in honor of another person was originally called "healths." Legend has it that a piece of bread was often placed on top of these honorary drinks—hence the word "toast."

- *Sidewalk manners:* Have you ever noticed that, when a man and woman from older generations are walking down a sidewalk together, the man usually walks on the outside (next to the street)? Before the age of indoor plumbing, pots of dirty water and other refuse were simply thrown out the window. The person walking next to the building was rarely drenched; the person next to the street was often not so lucky. Good manners instructed gentlemen to protect ladies from such unpleasant surprises and, thus, the man walked next to the street. To some extent, this custom and courtesy still remains with us today.

- *Sleeve buttons:* Even something as simple as the buttons on the sleeve of a man's coat has roots in the practice of etiquette. At one time, it was common practice to use your coat sleeve to wipe your mouth when eating. As the rules of etiquette developed, buttons were sewn onto sleeves as a reminder to use napkins. The buttons would cause sharp raps on offenders' noses if they used their sleeves across their mouths.

- *Pineapples:*   Legend has it that, after returning from a voyage, New England sea captains speared a pineapple on the iron gates in front of their homes to let it be known that they were home and all were welcome to visit. The pineapple has since been known as a symbol of hospitality and is still used as such in the northeast region of the United States. We don't have many such visible symbols today (because we only roll out the red carpet for visiting dignitaries), but an open door and a smiling face send a signal to others that they are welcome.

2. The basis of etiquette today

Do the old rules of etiquette still hold true today or have things really changed? Are there any basic foundations of appropriate behavior in business and social settings that have withstood the test of time? Changing attitudes in the business world—such as the globalization of the economy, an increasingly diverse workforce, and the electronic revolution—can terrify you regardless of how long you've been maneuvering in this setting. Business etiquette means more than knowing which utensil to use when. You have to know how to dress and how to interact with people in a variety of cultures. Knowing and practicing the fundamentals of etiquette are critical to your career success. It won't matter how smart or talented you are if you have faulty manners. You will be judged, perhaps unfairly, on your manners or the lack of them.

Today, the need to practice good manners is still important—but the need to know the basic rules of etiquette in a variety of different business and social settings is even more important. Not only are today's manners relatively simple to learn and practice, but they also indicate that a person is intelligent, confident, and considerate of fellow human beings. Understanding and practicing the basics of etiquette show that you care and desire to be taken seriously as a professional member of the business community.

Remember the little things. According to etiquette expert Letitia Baldrige, "Everyone has qualms when they're starting out in the business world. Even senior managers who have excelled in the workplace for decades confess to concern when plunged into strange, new territory, entering unknown situations, dealing with strangers about whom they know nothing other than their brief bios and some second-hand opinions." Therefore, the things we say and how we act and react toward others is an important part of business.

Be civil. "Civility" is one word that summarizes the most important aspect of etiquette in today's society. This word may seem to be a throwback to the imaginary days of old, but, in fact, it's more important now than ever before. Italian writers introduced the idea of civility when they advised against gossiping, boasting, pushing, and waving your arms while talking. Civility has since been defined as courteousness and is often used synonymously with politeness. Its practice today is probably more important than ever before. Recognizing the importance of civility in all of our actions is the first step in creating and maintaining enjoyable working and personal interactions.

- You can read and understand the rules of etiquette and even memorize what to do when, but, without treating others the way you would like to be treated—at work, home, and play—civility cannot flourish.

- Practicing civility creates an environment conducive to productivity and inclusiveness. It is evidenced in organizations by respect and good manners, and is as important as providing quality products, ensuring exceptional customer service, and achieving profitability. Courtesy and respect are recognized worldwide as characteristics of a true professional.

Follow the "Golden Rule."   No matter where your search of the history of etiquette takes you, similarities appear in developing societies. As Huston Smith points out in his classic text, *The World's Religions*, the foundation for maintaining good relationships in most cultures boils down to what Christians call the "Golden Rule":

- *Buddhism:*   Hurt not others in ways that you yourself would find hurtful.

- *Brahmanism:*   This is the sum of duty: Do naught unto others which would cause you pain if done to you.

- *Christianity:*   All things whatsoever ye would that men should do to you, do ye even to them.

- *Confucianism:*   What you do not like when done to yourself, do not do to others.

- *Islam:*   No one of you is a believer until he desires for his brother that which he desires for himself.

- *Taoism:*   Regard your neighbor's gain as your own gain, and your neighbor's loss as your own loss.

- *Zorastrianism:*   That nature alone is good which refrains from doing unto another whatsoever is not good for itself.

Don't try to be perfect.   Accidents and mistakes can happen anywhere and without notice—in your office, at a meeting, dining out, traveling, or anywhere you encounter supervisors, colleagues, or customers. What are they? Everything from missed appointments and deadlines, spilled coffee on a final report, or an inadvertedly shredded document to harsh words spoken in times of stress, incorrect information, inattention to details, and etiquette blunders may be upsetting and can create hard feelings. Fortunately, most people are willing to forgive unfortunate incidents and mistakes if you recognize them and apologize.

Not apologizing may result in resentment and distrust; negative working relationships may result. By apologizing and correcting mistakes, on the other hand, trust can be restored and positive working relationships can be maintained. Or, as Laura Yale says in "Manners Matter," "Frowns can be turned upside down with just a little effort."

Don't hold yourself up to perfection, and don't expect others to be perfect either. Beware of becoming a member of the etiquette police! These are people who relish knowing every little etiquette detail and correcting those whom they perceive to be in error. This, in itself, is a breach of manners. Remember that etiquette is based on civility and kindness, not on insisting on arcane etiquette rules.

In addition to knowing how to apologize gracefully, you need to use the following common words and phrases. If you are not already accustomed to using them, try them out and learn their power.

- "Please"
- "Thank you"
- "Excuse me"
- "May I help you?"

They are all short and simple, but when said with meaning, they convey respect.

Change with the times.   As you have seen from reading this chapter, some things stay the same, but others change with the times. Quaint practices of the past, such as the use of calling cards and women leaving the dinner table so men could have their after-dinner drinks, have faded from use. Some old rules—such as how we should dress in business settings—continue to evolve. And, brand-new etiquette rules—such as those for cell phones, email, and personal digital assistants (PDAs)—are always being added.

What can we learn from these changes? Be observant. Don't cling tenaciously to the rules of the past. Just because we have always done something a certain way doesn't mean we should continue to do it the same way in the future. We should be flexible and willing to learn new ways to fit with the changing times in which we live.

Beware of the generation gap. Speaking of changing with the times, communication expert Mary Munter has noted that it may be useful to think of two generations of people with whom you work: the Baby Boomers and the Boomers' Babies. Boomers' Babies tend to be: (1) multitaskers (perhaps talking to one person, instant messaging several others, and talking on their cell phone all at the same time) and (2) extremely informal (such as, addressing an email to a superior they don't know as "Hey Judith!" instead of "Dear Ms. White," using slang and curse words, and dressing very informally). Of course, not all people in the two generations behave this way and some people cross the generation lines (e.g., older people in high tech industries may behave more like Boomers' Babies and younger people in the banking industry behave more like Baby Boomers).

During your career, you will certainly have to work and behave like people in the Baby Boomer culture—because virtually all of the people who have the power to hire and promote you will be in that group. They will almost certainly interpret Boomers' Baby behavior as extremely rude in the business place. Therefore, always be sensitive to your audience: behave in the same way your superiors behave.

Be ethical.   Manners are important, but sometimes they seem to emphasize relatively superficial actions. The underlying issue of ethics is more important than issues like the intricacies of table settings. Ethics are concerned with the moral principles and values that govern how people, and even organizations, conduct their daily lives and activities. Although most people can easily distinguish between what they consider to be right or wrong, based on their own personal experiences, they are often faced with situations and decisions for which it is difficult to make those distinctions clearly. In an effort to promote ethical behavior, organizations often publish codes of ethics to help guide employees in their daily activities and decisions.

Even without the help of a code of ethics, one noted ethics expert, Stephen S. J. Hall, has identified some very simple questions you can ask yourself about any situation to identify ethical and unethical behavior.

- Will someone be hurt in this situation?
- Is anyone being coerced, manipulated, or deceived?
- Is there anything illegal about the situation?
- Does the situation feel wrong to you?
- Is someone else telling you that there is an ethical problem?
- Would you be ashamed to tell your best friend, your spouse, or your parents about your contemplated actions or your involvement?
- Do the outcomes, on balance, appear to be positive or negative?
- Do you or others have the right or duty to act in this situation?
- Is there a chance that you are denying or avoiding some serious aspect of the situation?

Finally, as noted earlier in this chapter, the simplest, yet most thorough, ethical guideline is the age-old Golden Rule: Do unto others as you would have them do unto you.

CHAPTER 2 OUTLINE

1. Dressing to make a good impression
   Guidelines for everyone
   Guidelines for men
   Guidelines for women

2. Introducing yourself and others
   Introducing yourself
   Introducing others
   Getting through awkward moments
   Using business cards
   Designing business cards
   Exchanging business cards
   Using name tags
   Responding to an introduction
   Standing for an introduction
   Making small talk
   Connecting with people
   Disengaging yourself

3. Shaking hands
   How to shake hands
   When to shake hands
   When to extend your hand
   When not to extend your hand

4. Interviewing basics
   Preparing for an interview
   Dressing for the interview
   Making a good impression
   Writing thank-you notes

CHAPTER 2

Creating a Powerful First Impression

As the old saying goes, "You never have a second chance to make a good first impression." Regardless of where you are (whether a sales call, client meeting, reception, or interview), be prepared to present yourself in a positive light, creating a powerful and lasting impression every time you meet someone. These first impressions will establish the tenor of the relationship. According to Susan Bixler and Nancy Nix-Rice, "Books are judged by their covers, houses are appraised by their curb appeal, and people are initially evaluated on how they choose to dress and behave. In a perfect world, this is not fair, moral, or just. What's inside should count a great deal more. And, eventually, it usually does, but not right away. In the meantime, a lot of opportunities can be lost." Everything, from the way you dress to how you handle introductions, creates first and lasting impressions.

Even if you have been in these situations before, mentally rehearse what to do before you step on stage. The script has been written and the parts have been cast. Do you know the script? What should your actions and lines be?

1. Dressing to make a good impression

Whether you like it or not, you are judged by the way you look. Long before you utter a word or extend your hand, opinions have been formed. The most important thing to remember about how to dress is to always dress to make your customers, clients, coworkers, or guests feel respected and comfortable. Don't forget that your choice of wardrobe could have an impact on your career. In fact, a good rule of thumb is to let your wardrobe reflect the position to which you aspire, not the position you currently hold. Whatever you choose to wear, keep it clean and neat.

Correct attire for business may vary by the situation and the culture. Therefore, the question of how you should dress to make the best impression in a variety of business settings can create some troublesome dilemmas. The first things you need to know are several common terms often used to note the type of dress that is expected. To help you demystify these terms, take a look at the following definitions:

- *Formal wear:*   Dinner jackets (tuxedos), evening gowns, or cocktail dresses.
- *Business attire:*   Suits with collared shirt and conservative ties or tailored dresses and suits with conservative blouses.
- *Business casual:*   Slacks with sports coat and button-up shirt or dresses and pant suits.
- *Dress-down day:*   Slacks or skirts (no shorts or well-worn denim) and shirts with collars or blouses (no tee-shirts or tank tops). Colleagues don't need to see belly buttons and/or biceps.

Opinions about appropriate on-the-job or off-the-job attire often vary by parts in different regions of the country, so—when in doubt—it is always a good idea to ask what is appropriate for the situation. What is considered business attire in California may not be viewed as such in New York City. In addition, most organizations have a dress code, whether published or not. When it involves your job, you should find out what it is and follow it. The following basics will let you play it safe when deciding what to wear and how to look:

Guidelines for everyone:

- Strive for a tailored and professional look.
- Solid colored shirts and blouses are a safe bet in almost every setting; don't mix stripes and patterns.

- The proper length of your suit or sport jacket should be about 3/4 inch longer than your thumb (when your arms are straight down).
- Sleeve cuffs should be approximately five inches from the tip of your thumb and show about one-half inch of material below the coat sleeve.
- Don't wear anything that can be identified with educational, social, political, or religious organizations.
- Don't wear sunglasses inside a building.
- Wear clean, polished shoes; never sneakers.
- Remove any facial or body piercings (excluding earnings for women) and wear clothes that cover any tattoos.
- Be freshly bathed and wear clean, wrinkle-free clothes.
- Stand and sit up straight; walk with pride and purpose in all that you do.

Guidelines for men:

- Wear a suit with a long-sleeved, collared shirt, and a conservative tie.
- Never let any shirt show between the tie and the waist of the pants.
- Choose a belt to blend with or match your shoes.
- Wear mid-calf socks so that your bare leg does not show when you cross your legs.
- If you wear a double-breasted suit, be sure to keep it buttoned.
- If you wear a hat, remove it as soon as you enter a building.
- Remove change and keys out of your pockets to avoid unsightly bulges and jingling noises.
- Be freshly shaved or trim facial hair neatly.

Guidelines for women:

- Create a professional image. For example, choose a solid suit and a conservative blouse.
- Always wear hose with skirts or dresses. Carry an extra pair with you in case you develop a run.
- Select hemlines and necklines with modesty and professionalism in mind.
- Carry a small portfolio, a purse, or both.
- Don't wear backless or open-toed shoes.
- Practice moderation when applying fragrances and makeup so that it is you who gets noticed—not the "extras" that you have added to your appearance.

2. Introducing yourself and others

Introducing yourself or others is a common business practice. Luckily, the rules of introductions are fairly simple. The first is to show respect for the most important person in the setting by mentioning that person's name first. The second is to try to include a brief comment about each person being introduced so that they have some basic knowledge of each other. These brief introductory statements provide opportunities to begin conversations as well as help associate names with faces, which improves name retention. It takes practice to remember names, but mastering this skill pays dividends as it builds meaningful relationships.

Introducing yourself: Often, you will need to introduce yourself. In these situations, simply approach the person you don't know, extend your hand, smile, and say, "Hello, I am Tien Chen Wang," adding something appropriate given the circumstances, such as "I'm the host's assistant," or "I'm here representing the City of Seattle." Take notice of your setting before introducing yourself and don't intrude on someone who is in conversation with another person.

When you see someone you have met before, help them remember you. Say something such as "Hi, Micah, I'm Khoon Koh with Asian-American Imports. We met at this conference in Hong Kong last year." This simple gesture takes the pressure off the other person, who may be trying to remember your name and place your face. It also provides a conversation starter. A typical response would be something simple like "Oh, yes, weren't those Chinese meals great?"

Introducing others: Introductions of people you know or to whom you would like to show special respect (such as your company president or your manager) have a special twist. The rule is to introduce the "less respected" person (lesser authority, rank, or age) to the "more respected" person (higher authority, rank, or age). In other words, say the "most respected" person's name first. As a matter of courtesy, clients should always be granted the status of holding the "most respected" position.

In addition, use titles to show respect and convey information to those whom you are introducing. Here are a few examples to show how this introduction hierarchy works:

- "Ms. Senior Executive, let me present Mr. Junior Executive. Mr. Junior Executive, this is Ms. Senior Executive."
- "Ms. Gonzales, I would like to introduce Letitia Cosby, who will help you complete the paperwork for your loan. Letitia, this is Ms. Gonzales."
- "Dean Dolphin, I would like you to meet Nicholas and Helena Mithras. Their son Alex will be attending our school this fall. Mr. and Mrs. Mithras, Dean Dolphin is the dean of the business school."

Getting through awkward moments: When it comes to introductions, there can be, and usually is, a little stress. What if you forget a name and get flustered? Do not worry. Your actions can alleviate the tension. If you forget someone's name, just say so. But help the other person by saying your name. This can be especially helpful if someone has forgotten or mispronounced your name. Your consideration may help them avoid a potentially embarrassing moment. In conversation, use the names of those around you. This will help those who may be meeting for the first time place names with faces.

Using business cards: These small, but powerful, pieces of paper serve as helpful tools to remember names and as information sources for follow-ups on professional and personal contacts. The wise use of business cards can be a great means of connecting you with others on a more personal basis.

Designing business cards:

- Chose a simple design. Have them printed on standard 3″ by 2″ card stock and be sure to include all of the following information: your name and title, company name, mailing address, fax number, email address, and phone number(s) (e.g., office, cell, and/or home phones).
- Don't get cute with your business cards. Remember that business cards are used for establishing contacts. Many people scan business cards into personal contact databases or file them in a card file for quick reference.

Exchanging business cards:

- Keep your cards handy, neat, and clean. The tattered or crumpled card you pull out of your wallet or purse sends the wrong message.
- Take a moment to study a business card when you are handed one. This simple gesture indicates your interest in the person.
- Lay the card on the table or desk in front of you. This allows you to keep names straight, especially if there are several people in the setting.
- Be sure to give a person one of your business cards if you are offered one, unless you are trying to discourage further contact. If you don't have business cards, it's okay to write your contact information on a piece of paper or on the back of the other person's card if they offer you this solution.

Using name tags: We wear name tags at business meetings and social events to make it easy to greet others and create conversations.

- Always be sure to place your name tag on your right shoulder, so that when you reach to shake hands, you can retain eye contact as you scan one another's name tags.
- Remember, the purpose of a name tag is to make greeting easier. Therefore, print your first and last name, making them big and bold.
- If the setting calls for it, print your title and the name of your organization.
- Refer to the name tag and use the person's name when you acknowledge an introduction.

Responding to an introduction: When you are introduced, you are expected to respond in some way.

- Make it a practice to add the name of the person you just met to whatever pleasantry you use. This helps you remember the person's name. However, don't overdo it by constantly repeating names. So after being introduced, you might say, "How do you do, Ms. Trujillo?" or "I am pleased to meet you, Ms. Trujillo."
- Be sure to smile and make eye contact when you respond to an introduction.
- Whatever the setting, always remember to treat everyone you meet, from the janitor to the president, with the same respect.
- Speak clearly. Slurred names are hard to understand.

Standing for an introduction: Today, men and women stand when they are being introduced—regardless of whether the other person is a man or a woman. In a business situation, it is especially respectful to stand when a client enters your workspace. Well-mannered business men and women often come around their desk and shake hands with clients before getting down to business. However, if you work together or see each other often, there is no need to stand every time a colleague enters your work space.

Making small talk: Small talk—that idle chit-chat that seems so easy with friends and colleagues—is often difficult with strangers.

• When it is time to strike up a conversation, making a comment about the weather may not be as "hokey" as it at first appears. Such simple comments serve as icebreakers, so stick to subjects that make it easy for everyone to comment on or to join the conversation.

• Stay current on a variety of topics, from late-breaking news and sports to the arts and best sellers. Then, no matter what the setting, you will be ready to start or join conversations.

• Another way to establish rapport is to find common interests or acquaintances with the people you meet. Be observant for cues in offices or other business settings, such as pictures, plaques, trophies, and other mementoes that might serve as conversation starters.

• One sure way to kill a conversation or turn off people is to bring up issues concerning politics or religion, because these may touch emotional nerves. The same holds true of personal health issues, marital problems, rumors, gossip, and money.

Connecting with people: Mastering the art of mingling is very important to most careers; you never know what doors may open because of your ability to mingle. Therefore, at business gatherings, make sure you talk with as many people as possible.

• When striking up conversations with people you don't know, take a discrete look at their name tags, look them in the eye, offer a firm handshake, and say, "Hello, I'm Miguel Cozamel" and follow up with a comment that tells something about you.

- Make sure that the person with whom you are speaking receives your full attention. Whether speaking with one person or a group, the rudest thing you can do is look around as if looking for someone "more important" with whom to speak.

- Finally, practice good listening skills (as described on page 45). You'll soon learn that good listeners also make good conversationalists because they tune in to those around them. Even if you find the conversation boring, keep listening; you may be surprised at what you learn. Be enthusiastic and show your interest by maintaining eye contact and asking questions. If you are having trouble involving people in conversations, ask questions that lead them to talk about themselves or ask for their opinions of appropriate matters. Then, your listening skills can come into play.

Disengaging yourself: At some point, conversations will come to a natural end. Look for cues when it is time to move on and make a graceful exit. Simple comments like the following will let you move on effortlessly:

- "Pardon me, I need to speak with Priscilla before she leaves."
- "Excuse me while I say hello to Lindsay."
- "Let me introduce you to Conrad."

Even if the conversation is spellbinding, you still need to keep moving and interacting with different people. When you find yourself in business-related conversations that need to be continued, offer your business card and say you will call later.

3. Shaking hands

Handshakes are the norm in the western world, so be prepared to shake hands in business settings. In other cultures, however, handshakes may only be part of an introduction; you'll learn more about when to extend or not extend your hand in international settings in Chapter 8. Just as people size you up based on your appearance, they will make judgments about your handshake and when and how you use it. Because this gesture of connectivity is so common, knowing and practicing a little handshake etiquette will put you and others at ease.

How to shake hands:

- Extend your right hand with your thumb up.
- Shake firmly but considerately. Gauge your handshake to the strength of the person whose hand you are shaking.
- Pump the other person's hand once or twice.
- Break from the handshake quickly after a few seconds. Do not continue to hold the other person's hand during the entire introduction.
- Make eye contact with the person, but do not stare.
- Always keep your drink in your left hand. That way you never have to fumble around to shake hands or, even worse, extend a cold and clammy hand.

When to shake hands: In general, shake hands when you are:

- Meeting someone for the first time,
- Meeting someone you have not seen in a long time,
- Greeting your host or hostess,
- Greeting your guests, or
- Saying goodbye when you want to show extra respect.

When to extend your hand:

- In almost any business setting, a handshake is always appropriate—whether it's man-to-man, woman-to-man, or woman-to-woman. (Until recently, it was considered impolite for a man to extend his hand to a woman, but that is no longer true in business.)
- However, if there are dignitaries or much higher-ranked executives present, you should wait for them to extend their hands.

- Always shake hands with anyone who extends his or her hand to you, no matter what the situation. It is extremely rude to ignore or refuse to shake hands when someone offers a hand to you.
- As you extend your hand, make eye contact, smile, and say "How do you do?" "Hello."
- If you extend your hand and the other person doesn't respond, simply withdraw your hand and continue talking.

When not to extend your hand:

- If the other person's hands are full, simply nod your head and say something like "Hello," or "It's nice to see you again."
- If you approach a dignitary or someone of obviously higher rank, wait for that person to extend a hand first.
- If someone says he or she is sick and would prefer not to shake hands, it is okay to dispense with the formality.

4. Interviewing basics

Nowhere are first impressions more important than in a job interview setting. You are on stage from the moment you enter the job search process. Whether unemployment rates are high or low, employers are always seeking to attract the best talent. Take the necessary steps to set yourself apart from others in the interviewing crowd and be recognized as the best. Remember, in the job search process, you are competing with other applicants as you attempt to sell your knowledge, skills, and abilities to a targeted and informed audience—a prospective employer.

You can conduct much of the initial job search process at a distance through employment agencies, networking, letter writing, emails, and telephone calls. Each of these contacts—from your cover letter and résumé to telephone calls and emails—creates an impression of your qualifications, as well as your level of interest and attention to detail, setting the stage for success. However, the most important hiring decision usually depends on a face-to-face encounter: the personal interview.

Preparing for an interview: As you prepare to sell yourself in the interview process,

- Read and learn all you can about your prospective employer and what they do. Show that you are informed.

- Think about your work-related achievements and how you can make them come to life with concrete examples.

- Take the time to practice answering questions before you arrive at an interview. Try to anticipate the questions an interviewer might ask. Ask a friend or associate to conduct a mock interview with you. Remember, during the interview, you are on stage: the interview is show time—not the time for a dress rehearsal.

- Be prepared to answer thought-provoking questions (such as those listed here) to demonstrate your personal preparation and familiarity with the job and the organization: (1) What skills could you bring to our organization? (2) Why do you want to work for us? (3) What do you see yourself doing for our organization in five years? (4) Who was the most difficult person you ever worked with, and why was he or she difficult to work with? (5) What is your greatest weakness, and what have you done to overcome it? (6) How do you plan to achieve your career goals? (7) Which is more important to you, salary or the type of job? (8) What have you learned from your mistakes? (9) How has your education prepared you for your career? (10) Is there anything else I should know about you?

Dressing for the interview: Before going to an interview, find out how people dress where you will be interviewing. When the interview is being scheduled, ask how you should dress. Otherwise, when in doubt, you can never go wrong by slightly overdressing for an interview.

- In any case, unless the atmosphere is very relaxed, a business suit with a pressed white shirt and a tie is always safe for men.

- Women should wear a solid colored, knee-length skirt with a tailored blouse and pumps.

- If you are told not to dress up, a neatly pressed shirt or blouse and pants or skirt would be appropriate.

- Leave your briefcase at home. Instead, take a file folder or portfolio containing several copies of your résumé and some paper for notes. Your résumé may not have been given to everyone you will meet; this is a great tool for helping people remember your name and it serves as a conversation starter.

Making a good impression: In the interview setting, first impressions are crucial. You may be the perfect person for the job, but research shows that if you don't create a powerful first impression on the interviewer, you may not get the job—regardless of your abilities. Remember, the organization at which you are interviewing is seeking the best employee from a qualified pool of applicants. In other words, they are attempting to eliminate candidates in their quest to fill the position. Don't be eliminated from consideration by your timing, dress, posture, or handshake.

- Demonstrate enthusiasm and respect by arriving a few minutes early. Show your respect for others by respecting their time. Plan to arrive before the scheduled appointment; however, if you arrive more than ten or fifteen minutes early, tell the receptionist that you do not want to disturb your host and will wait until the scheduled time. Be sure to leave extra time between appointments for unexpected delays.

- Introduce yourself to the first person you meet, tell them why you are there, and ask for directions to the person you are scheduled to meet. Don't forget that everyone is an interviewer. Even the receptionist who greets you may be forming an impression of you as you sit in the waiting area. Never be casual; always assume you are being observed.

- Show your interest in the job by reading company literature, trade publications, or professional journals—not the latest sports or glamour magazine.

- At the beginning and end of each interview, wait until the person in charge extends a hand and then follow the previously-discussed rules for shaking hands. Don't worry if your hand is a little damp. Nervousness can create sweaty palms and it only shows that you are truly excited about the job prospect. However, if your hand is really moist, discretely wipe it on your pants or skirt before shaking hands.

- Walk confidently as you move through the interview process from one person to the next. Sit up straight at all times, even when you are not being interviewed. Maintain eye contact with the person conducting the interview and provide brief but complete answers to all questions.

- Think before you answer questions. Once you have given an answer; there is no way to take back what you said.

- Simple "yes" or "no" answers to questions don't give any clues to the interviewer about your knowledge, skills, or abilities. When responding to questions, take the opportunity to explain how you can benefit your future employer.

- As you answer questions, take time to think about questions you want answered. This is your opportunity to learn more about the organization and the job for which you are applying.

As excited as you might be, relax, smile, and follow the interviewer's lead. Don't continue to talk after the interviewer has obtained all the needed information. To signal the end of the interview, interviewers will typically ask if you have any questions. Be prepared for what you will say and ask any questions you may have about the organization and/or the position. After dealing with your questions and concerns, interviewers typically rise, extend their hands, and tell you that they will be in touch.

Writing thank-you notes: At the time of the interview, you should always thank your interviewer for their time and the opportunity of exploring how you might fit into their organization. However, a verbal "thank you" is not enough. When you begin the interview process, jot down the names and titles of everyone involved. Once you return from interviewing, write a short thank-you note to each of these individuals.

- Address your letter to the key person (include his or her title) who handled your visit.

- Begin by thanking them for their time and reminding them who you are and for what position you applied.

- Next, tell them why you want the job and how your skills and abilities will contribute to the organization's success. If you forgot to highlight anything important about your qualifications during the interview, do it now. Tell the person that you would like to become a member of their organization.

- Include a comment from your interview that personalizes your message.

- Finally, close by saying you are looking forward to hearing from them soon and, if appropriate, that you are enclosing any requested materials.

If you don't hear from a prospective employer after you send a thank-you letter, it's okay to follow up with one telephone call. It shows that you are persistent, interested, and enthusiastic about the opportunity. However, don't be impatient. Wait a couple of weeks and then call, but not on Monday, the most hectic day of the workweek.

For more information on interviewing, please see *Guide to Interpersonal Communication,* cited on page 111.

CHAPTER 3 OUTLINE

1. Conflict resolution
   Learn to control yourself
   Attempt to understand the other person
   Don't problem solve too soon

2. Personal workspace
   Before entering
   After entering

3. Office romances
   Definitely don't . . .
   Probably okay . . .
   In any case, be discreet

4. Business travel
   Taking the "war" out of road warrior
   Planning ahead
   Dealing with service employees
   Dealing with seatmates

5. Other potential conflict situations
   Dealing with a difficult supervisor
   Working with a new supervisor
   Dealing with office politics

CHAPTER 3

Maintaining Business Relationships

Although creating powerful first impressions sets the stage to develop positive business relationships, it takes work to maintain those relationships. Everyday roadblocks and pitfalls—from conflicts and office politics to the stresses of business travel and office romances—can quickly create tension and dissension. Learning to identify and deal with situations where conflict can impede both your career and your organization's success is a real test of your etiquette skills.

I. Conflict resolution

If we always worked with completely congenial colleagues and customers, work life would be simple. Alas, however, such perfection is elusive. Because you will eventually encounter conflict at work, you must learn to manage it. The following suggestions will help improve your conflict management skills.

Learn to control yourself.

- Create a climate that fosters open communication in which people feel comfortable asking questions, discussing ideas, and resolving issues so that everyone wins.

- Keep your emotions in check. Although it is easier said than done, try not to lose your temper. Breathe deeply and exhale, letting your emotions escape. Do not waste your emotional resources by being mad or plotting revenge.

- Do not resort to threats or attempt to force people to agree with you. Appeal to common goals that everyone can strive to achieve.

- If feelings are running high, walk away or offer to call back later so you and/or the other person can "cool off."

- Tap the power of silence. Don't interrupt, and avoid the temptation to fill in during pauses. Use the time to compose yourself and listen carefully.

- Never be condescending, even if you think the other person caused the problem.

- Choose your battles wisely. You may win in the short run but lose in the long run. People will avoid listening to and working with you if they perceive you as combative and always having to win.

- Learn to accept criticism. Remember that most criticism is not aimed at you as a person; it is aimed at a specific behavior in a specific situation. Even if it does seem personal, try to think of it as situation-specific.

Attempt to understand the other person.

- Avoid being judgmental.

- Try to create win/win solutions. Listen closely to what the other person is saying and seek agreement by searching for common ground and mutual understanding. Accentuate the positive by focusing on issues, not on personalities. Incorporate others' ideas and suggestions to make it easy for them to say "yes."

- Ask questions, and paraphrase to make sure you understand the other person's position and feelings.
- Recognize their valid points. Other people can also have workable solutions.
- Empathize by putting yourself in the other person's shoes. If you do not empathize, you may not identify or understand their interests or intent. Looking at problems based solely on your experiences provides little common ground for mutual understanding.
- Keep a close eye on your body language. Subconscious actions such as crossing your arms and losing eye contact can hamper open communication.
- Use "minimal encouragers" like nods, smiles, and simple comments to demonstrate you are listening and truly engaged.
- Allow the person to vent for a few minutes, if appropriate. Sometimes their ranting is nothing personal, it's just a way to relieve frustration.

Don't problem solve too soon.

- Be sure you understand what's on their minds before you offer unsolicited advice or quick-fix solutions.
- Do not push too hard or fast for agreement. Sometimes speed leads people to believe that you are neither listening to nor understanding them.

2. Personal workspace

A special challenge to maintaining business relationships and resolving conflict involves personal workspace. In today's open environment, remember four walls and a door may not define an office; personal work areas can range all the way from private offices, to cubicles, to desks and shared workspaces. Whatever the design or location, they all have one thing in common: they are designed for work. Avoid the bad manners associated with encroachment; observe the following workspace courtesies:

Before entering:

* Think of someone's work area as personal space. Treat it with the same respect you would expect in your workspace.

* Knock or pause before you enter a private office, even if you have an appointment.

* If the person is on the phone, always wait until the call is finished before entering.

* When your visit takes you to a cubicle, treat the location just like a private office. Don't peer over the side or barge right in, even though there isn't a door.

* When desks are arranged in an open or landscaped environment, treat each person's workspace as personal space.

* Respect your coworkers' work areas by avoiding interruptions and actions that could take away from their productivity. In open work areas, it is especially important to remember to talk softly so you don't disturb others.

After entering:

* If you are an infrequent visitor to a coworker's office, wait until asked before sitting down.

* Don't move anything or spread your papers on anyone else's desk.

* Don't stand over people's backs while working with them at their desk, lean over them to point at work on their desk, or read their computer screens.

* Excuse yourself if the person needs to take a phone call.

* Keep your visit short and to the point.

3. Office romances

The issue of office romances provides yet another challenge for maintaining relationships. In decades past, many organizations had strict policies against amorous relationships at work; some organizations still define limits (for example, who may date whom). However, office romances are definitely more pervasive now than they have been in the past. It is no longer uncommon to meet one's mate in the work environment since the workplace is a nonthreatening venue to get to know others well. Additionally, coworkers already have one "big thing" in common—work—and may have many other similar interests and backgrounds. One expert on office relations asserts that the success rate of relationships originating in the office is higher than with any other means of meeting.

However, office romance has its down side. The biggest danger of office romance is the potential for charges of sexual harassment. More common problems include office gossip, perception of favoritism by other workers, and uncomfortable situations following break-ups. You can limit your risks and increase your likelihood for success by following some simple guidelines, ranging from *definitely don't* to *probably okay*.

Definitely don't . . .

- *Date any married coworker:*   Such affairs are too likely to "burn" you emotionally and professionally.

- *Date a direct supervisor or subordinate:*   Any relationship between a boss and a direct subordinate can lead to negative consequences—from legal actions to damaged careers.

- *Be a flirt:*   In this day and age, flirting with coworkers can result, at worst, in a sexual harassment suit, and at the very least, in your being taken less seriously as a professional. To steer clear of office flirting, dress modestly at work, limit physical contact to warm handshakes, minimize your intake of alcohol at office parties and functions, and stay away from the mistletoe at the holiday party!

- *Become a "serial dater":*   Think of your workplace as a small town. No matter how discreet you think you are, word will spread if you date several coworkers at one time or several in quick succession.

- *Engage in sexual harassment:*   Sexual harassment is repeated, unwelcome sexual advances; requests for sexual favors; and any other verbal remarks or physical contact of a sexual nature. Such conduct is illegal when it . . .

1. Is made either explicitly or implicitly as a condition of employment decisions.
2. Has the purpose or effect of unreasonably interfering with an individual's work performance, and/or
3. Creates an intimidating, hostile, or offensive working environment.

Therefore, beware of saying or doing anything that could be considered sexual in nature. Forget about telling off-color jokes and leave the "cheese cake" and "beef cake" calendars at home.

Probably okay . . .

- *Date a colleague:*   Dating a colleague is less problematic than dating the boss, but can still lead to problems if the relationship sours and you must continue to work closely together. Take time to get to know a coworker before dating. Going out to lunch or dinner after work makes for a comfortable transitional step to dating.

- *Date an employee in another department:*   Dating a colleague with whom you do not work on a frequent basis will probably lead to the fewest pitfalls of office romance.

In any case, be discreet.   Work is still the primary focus of any workplace; on the job, you should treat each other as coworkers, not "significant others." Remember to focus your work-time attention on the job at hand—no lengthy phone chats, frequent instant messaging, well-timed trips to the vending machine, or lingering lunches. Refrain from public displays of affection at work. Also, do not use the company email system to send love notes! Remember that these amorous thoughts can become permanent records.

4. Business travel

Maintaining business relationships as you travel can also be difficult. All too often, job demands and the uncertainties of travel lead to stress and frustration. Unfortunately, this stress and frustration can lead, in turn, to outbursts of temper directed at front-line service personnel, creating a "mad at the world" mood that can spill over into everything you do. Learning to cope with the unexpected can keep you in a positive frame of mind for effective etiquette for business travel.

Taking the "war" out of road warrior: Business and professional travel can bring out the best or the worst in people. If everything goes as planned, life on the road can be tolerable, or even enjoyable, as you establish business relationships and chronicle interesting stories. However, as you start racking up miles, the best-laid plans can often go awry, making a demanding and stress-filled job more difficult. Many of these confrontations, and their negative fallout, could be avoided if travelers recognize the importance of manners in all encounters.

Planning ahead: To lessen stress, look at your schedule. Who will you be seeing? What will you be doing? What types of clothing will you need?

- Sometimes it helps to make a list of clothing needs before you even start packing. Then, as you pack, check each item off your list. This helps avoid the nagging feeling that you left something behind.
- Schedule enough time for layovers to avoid nerve-racking, mad dashes to catch connecting flights.
- Leave time after long flights to clean up or take a quick nap. When you feel rested and well groomed, it shows.

Dealing with service employees: Remember, front-line service employees are not necessarily responsible for your problems. As simple as it may sound when you are not in the heat of the moment, approach the problem as a partner seeking a solution, not as an adversary. You will be surprised at how often service personnel will go out of their way to help you.

- Start the search for solutions by explaining your problem in a nonconfrontational fashion.

- Ask if there is some way that the situation can be resolved in a manner that will work for both of you.

- Finally, even if everything is not resolved to your satisfaction, always thank service personnel for their efforts.

- Remain pleasant in order to yield the biggest dividends. Yelling, screaming, and cursing may relieve your frustrations, but they will reflect badly on you and your organization.

Dealing with seatmates: Unless it is your first time to be shoe horned into a crowded airplane, you are already painfully aware of one of the more awkward situations in airline travel—the intrusive seatmate.

- No, you do not have to talk to the person sitting next to you when you travel. However, if you don't want to talk, there's no need to be rude. Simply occupy yourself: read a magazine, newspaper, or book; do your work; or put on your headset—even if you're not listening to anything.

- By the same token, if your seatmate has given you indications that he or she does not want to talk, don't persist in striking up a conversation.

5. Other potential conflict situations

Three other situations may also test your ability to maintain good business relationships—dealing with a difficult supervisor, a new supervisor, and office politics.

Dealing with a difficult supervisor: If you feel you have the "boss from hell," think long and hard about how much he or she deserves the title. Just because you have to be at work on time, only take authorized breaks, perform quality work, and interact successfully with pleasant and not-so-pleasant clients and coworkers does not mean you are being abused at work. However, there are unreasonable supervisors you just can't please, regardless of what you say or do. When you find yourself in this situation, there are things you can do to make your work life a little better.

- Don't let frustration get to you. Continue to do your job to the best of your abilities.

- Don't take criticism personally. As with any conflict situation, don't let your emotions control your actions.

- Document the behavior of your supervisor when actions are out of order, such as sexual harassment or overtime abuses, and give this information to the appropriate person in the human resources department.

- Always take the opportunity to clarify expectations, especially during formal performance evaluations. Attempt to open the lines of communication.

- Take a hard look at yourself to see if your supervisor may have good reasons for being so critical.

- Keep your résumé current; it can provide a great deal of comfort because you never know when you might want to change jobs.

- If the situation seems hopeless, find another job before quitting the one you have. It's easier to find a job when you are employed than when you are not.

Dealing with office politics: Office politics are a part of work life in which you will be involved sooner or later. Politics are powerful, and the quest for power at work can lead to problems. Office gossip, like politics, is just a part of work. A little gossip can be intriguing, but it can quickly go too far and can not only harm but also destroy relationships. Here are some steps you can take to limit potential damage to yourself and your career.

- Help your organization and coworkers achieve positive goals.

- Be positive in all of your interactions. Create a professional image by avoiding whining and complaining.

- Don't criticize or belittle coworkers. Don't try to make them look bad.

- Make it clear to those with whom you work that you do not want to be part of office gossip. Prove it by not spreading it.

- Don't burn your bridges behind you by making enemies or developing a reputation as a trouble maker. Getting your way through intimidation may work for a while, but it backfires sooner or later.

- Leave your personal problems at home. Anything you discuss at work probably won't remain a secret for long.

CHAPTER 4 OUTLINE

1. Communication etiquette
   Audience
   Clear purpose
   Channel choice

2. Face-to-face etiquette
   Being a good listener
   Communicating nonverbally

3. Telephone etiquette
   Telephone voice
   Telephone greetings
   Taking calls
   Cell telephones
   Speaker phones
   Leaving messages
   Returning calls

4. Writing etiquette
   Specific recipient
   Business letters
   Memos (memorandums)
   Reports
   Faxes (facsimiles)
   Editing issues
   Proofread

5. Email etiquette
   Composing email
   Processing email

6. Web page etiquette

7. Public speaking etiquette
   Practice
   Speeches
   Preparing
   Delivery
   Question-and-answer sessions

CHAPTER 4

Communication Etiquette

Your message light is blinking; your computer screen is filled with unread emails; several letters are sitting on your desk; the phone rings; and a colleague appears from nowhere holding a folder full of papers. Sound familiar? If you are like most business people, you spend more time on communication than on any other job activity.

Business people have always spoken to people face-to-face and in groups, and sent and received written documents. In today's world, however, we also have email, voicemail, faxes, videoconferencing, and more to deal with. In all of these interactions—whether traditional or electronic—we must learn how to put our best foot forward. Following some basic rules of etiquette will add a professional touch to your contacts and help you become more effective in these essential activities.

I. Communication etiquette

Some rules of business communication etiquette will be similar in all settings: for example, proper grammar and form are basic to all communication. Most importantly, however, all business communication is based on clarity about your audience and purpose.

Audience: Good communication is, first of all, a matter of reaching your targeted audience in a professional manner. Therefore, the question to ask yourself is "Who is my intended audience?" Your audience could range all the way from a coworker or a client to a government agency or a supplier. Thinking in terms of who will be receiving your message will dictate your channel choice and the style and tone of the message (such as an informal phone call versus a formal letter). For any style, however, (1) avoid jargon unless it is a time saver or is understood by your audience and (2) choose your words, level of detail, and approach to fit the educational background and familiarity of your reader with the subject. Don't put people down by communicating above their heads and don't be condescending by targeting your message below them.

Clear purpose: You have an obligation to your audience to be specific in all of your communication. If you want information, ask for it. If you need to apologize, do it and offer atonement for the mistake. If you want a job interview, ask for it. Too often, message receivers are left wondering, "Why did we have this conversation?" or "Why did I get this memo?" Respect the audience's time. When you call, state your purpose right away. Likewise, tell your readers why they are receiving correspondence from you in the attention line, subject line, or first paragraph. In business, "time is money," so keep your message short and follow the rules of etiquette for your selected channel.

Channel choice: All communication involves decisions not only about audience and purpose, but also some thought about channel choice (such as writing, emailing, or speaking). Your choice of channel will dictate the etiquette rules to follow. For example, face-to-face communication—with voice tone variations, body language, and the opportunity for instant feedback—requires a different set of manners than composing and sending a formal letter. Let's look at what is involved in making a professional statement with each communication option. When choosing a channel, first consider these factors:

- Should you be formal or informal?
- Do you need to hear and/or see a person's reactions?
- Do you need an immediate response or can you wait?
- Do you need to elicit high audience participation or not?
- Do you need a channel that appeals to just a few—or all—of the receiver's senses?
- Do you need a permanent record of this communication?

According to communication expert Mary Munter, once you have answered these questions, then you can consider the advantages and disadvantages of each channel in order to make your final selection. Choose carefully and make sure you use the appropriate channel for your audience and the recipient's cultural context. (Once you have chosen your channel, refer to the techniques covered in the rest of the chapter.)

- *Face to face:*   Advantages include immediate feedback, the ability to note body language, spontaneity, and the personal touch that comes through conversations. Disadvantages include the use of time and money, the possibility of unpleasant encounters, an inability to control the flow of conversation, and the lack of a permanent record.
- *Telephone:*   Advantages include immediate feedback, the ability to hear voice tone, the possibility of including several people at different locations, spontaneity, and a bit of a personal touch. Disadvantages include not being able to see body language, inability to control the flow of conversation, and no permanent record.
- *Traditional writing:*   Advantages include precise wording, as much detail as desired, privacy, and a permanent record. Disadvantages include delayed transmission time, no control over when (or even if) the message is received, delayed response, and a possible lack of flexibility.
- *Facsimile (fax):*   The advantages and disadvantages are basically the same as traditional writing. However, an additional advantage is faster transmission time and an additional disadvantage could be a lack of privacy.
- *Email:*   Advantages include those of traditional writing with a few additions: more likely to be spontaneous and creative, less likely to take as much "prep" time, easy for the audience to respond quickly, and easy to send to multiple audiences simultaneously. Disadvantages could include being hard to read because it is less likely to be well-edited, becoming the

property of the organization, possible use in lawsuits, and permanency (cannot be erased or shredded).

- *Web pages:*   Advantages include 24/7 access, ability to enhance through graphics and sound, ability to reach people you don't know, and links to related information. Disadvantages include being impersonal (because simple Web pages are forms of one-way communication, not directed to a specific person, and readers must instigate further communication).

- *Public speaking:*   Advantages include providing the same message to large numbers of people at one time, appealing to multiple senses through animation, sound, sight, and body language, controlling when the message is received, and interactive responses. Disadvantages include gathering the audience in one place, limiting the amount of detail provided, and possibly being speaker centered.

2. Face-to-face etiquette

You've already learned the basics of greetings and introductions in Chapter 2. However, whether your encounters are with one person or as a speaker to a group, face-to-face communication involves a lot more. With face-to-face communication, you are literally visible during the interaction. Everything you do and say carries a meaning. Simple things such as a laugh, smile, shrug, frown, or yawn send a message. Your actions can either reinforce your message or detract from it; make sure your actions send the right message.

Being a good listener: One of the most powerful and engaging tools of a good face-to-face communicator is the art of listening. Practice the skill of listening as much as you do the art of speaking. The following actions all show you are engaged and intent on listening.

- Focus your attention on the person with whom you are speaking.
- Maintain an open posture: don't cross your arms or look rigid.
- Make eye contact to signal interest and involvement.
- Eliminate physical barriers by moving from behind desks and podiums. Avoid distractions like phone calls or interruptions.
- Nod with understanding.
- Ask questions for clarification and encourage others to speak.
- Paraphrase to communicate your understanding.
- Stop talking and let the other person speak.
- Avoid yawning. If you can't suppress the urge to yawn, simply turn or lower your head and cover your mouth with your hand.

Communicating nonverbally: The fact that you can see and be seen by others in face-to-face communication is both good and bad: if you send the right nonverbal signals, you can improve communication; however, if you send the wrong signals, you can impede your message.

- In the office, keep a comfortable distance of four to eight feet between you and those with whom you are working; in conversation, keep a comfortable distance of about one and a half to two feet.
- Keep your posture natural. Avoid distracting movements such as rocking, leg swinging, or tapping.

- Smile when appropriate and use relaxed and interested facial expressions.
- Use hand gestures to animate your thoughts, but don't overdo it.

Just as you should be aware of your own nonverbal messages, take note of those that are sent to you.

- If the person with whom you are talking leans away from you, you're too close for comfort. If that person is leaning toward you, then you may be a little too far away.
- If someone is rigid and closed off (arms crossed against chest), try to find out why that person is uncomfortable or displeased.
- If other people lack eye contact or keep glancing at their watches, they may be uninterested in what you are saying. Perhaps you should cut the conversation short.

For more information on face-to-face etiquette, see the *Guide to Interpersonal Communication*, cited on page 111.

3. Telephone etiquette

Poise and professionalism are also communicated through proper telephone manners. How you handle yourself on the phone says a lot about you and the organization for which you work.

Telephone voice: When speaking on the telephone, these helpful hints will make you more effective.

* Speak clearly, directly into the receiver, and enunciate carefully.

* Don't be distracted by other work or chew gum while on the phone. This lack of respect is transferred to the other end of the line, even though the person can't see you.

* Speak just a bit more slowly than you would if you were talking with someone face-to-face.

* If you need to find information for a caller while he or she is on the line, put the caller on hold.

* Offer to phone the caller back if you need to place him or her on hold for more than a minute.

* Always try to smile when you speak; your warmth and sincerity will come through to the person with whom you are speaking.

Telephone greetings: When you answer an incoming call from outside your place of business, start with a greeting and then identify yourself. For instance, you might say, "Good morning. John Smith speaking," or "Thank you for calling Hinkle and Sweeney. This is Chris. How may I help you?" If you know the call is internal to your organization, simply state your name.

Taking calls: Remember, when you are in a meeting or with someone, it is never polite to answer the phone. If possible, have your calls picked up by an answering machine or forwarded to an associate. If, however, you are expecting an important call, alert people at the start of the meeting that you are expecting a call you must take and apologize when you do take the call.

Cell telephones: Cell phones are wonderful devices that provide incredible freedom of movement: no longer do you need to be tethered to one physical location; cell phones allow you to be contacted anywhere, at any time. However, when your cell phone rings in the wrong setting, it can be a distraction, an irritant, or downright inconsiderate.

- Be conscious of the fact that you are carrying a cell phone. When you are with someone, treat him or her with respect by turning off or not answering your phone.
- Don't be rude. Instead, rely on the messaging function and return these calls when you are away from individual contacts or group settings.
- Unless you are expecting a critical, time-sensitive call, your cell phone should always be turned off before all business meetings.

Speaker phones: With the availability of comfortable, quality headsets, speaker phones are no longer needed to free your hands for work. They are, however, useful for including others in important conversations.

- As a courtesy, always let the person on the other end of the call know that you are using a speaker phone.
- Respect the other person on the call by not doing any work while on the phone.
- Introduce all the people in the room and explain why they are included in the call, even if they will not participate.
- Do not use your speakerphone to listen to your voicemail. Playing them on the speakerphone, even when the volume is muted, can be distracting to those around you.

Leaving messages: When leaving a message by voicemail . . .

- Be brief and to the point; enunciate clearly.
- Give your name, telephone number, and reason for calling.
- State what time would be best to return your call.
- Repeat your phone number at the conclusion of your message. To make sure the other person has time to write it down, state the area code (pause), the first three numbers (pause), and then the last four numbers. Then repeat the entire number once more, quickly.
- Keep in mind that voicemail is a recording. Many a message has been played back time and time again, much to the chagrin of people who left their thoughts in haste. In addition, voicemail may be forwarded to others.

Returning calls: A final telephone etiquette point: when you tell someone you will call back right away or by a certain time, be sure to fulfill your promise. Develop a system that will allow you to respond to all messages within one business day. The same holds true for voicemail messages; they should also be returned within one business day.

4. Writing etiquette

You will encounter many traditional forms of written communication throughout your business career: letters, reports, memos, and faxes. All business writing should be clear and most should be succinct. The following tips will let you stand out in your business writing:

Specific recipient: If possible, always address your writing to a specific person. If you do not know the person, make a call or search the organization's web site to get a specific name and title as well as to verify correct spelling. Never use first names with people higher in rank or importance, unless they invite you to do so. When in doubt, use Mr., Ms., or Dr. (if appropriate).

Business letters: Use letters for external communication. If there is no printed company letterhead, then include (1) an inside return address followed by the date, (2) a salutation, (3) the body of the message, and (4) a complimentary close (such as "Sincerely"), and your signature.

Memos (memorandums): Use memos for internal communication. Always include five key items: (1) the addressee (the "to" line), (2) the sender (the "from" line), (3) the date written (the "date" line), (4) a subject line, and (5) the message itself. Finally, sign or initial your memos to indicate that you have read what is written.

Reports: Use reports to present extensive research and recommendations. The contents of the report should include: (1) title page, (2) table of contents, (3) executive summary, (4) introduction, (5) methodology (if applicable), (6) conclusions or recommendations, and (7) appendices and exhibits (if applicable). In addition, always include a cover letter explaining the purpose, scope, and limits of the report as well as appropriate acknowledgments. For more information on report writing, see the *Guide to Report Writing*, cited on page 111.

Faxes (facsimiles): Treat faxes like any other professional business correspondence. Use a cover sheet and be forewarned that faxes are usually not confidential unless the receiving machine is in a secure location.

Editing issues: According to communication expert Mary Munter, both "macro" and "microissues" should be addressed for effective written communication.

Macroediting (the document as a whole):

- Write with "high skim value." Use headings and subheadings to enable busy readers to skim your document for important points.

- Use structural signposts for connection. Use document design or transitional words to make the connection and logical flow between your ideas clear.

- Compose effective paragraphs or sections. Each paragraph needs a topic sentence and supporting sentences.

Microediting (sentences and words):

- Avoid using unnecessary words and overly long sentences.

- Use a suitable style (formal or informal, businesslike or bureaucratic, jargon or no jargon).

Proofread: Before you send out any document, show respect for your reader by always taking the time to proofread for correct grammar, spelling, and content. Remember that all writing can become a permanent record. You can never take it back, and your writing reflects on you.

For more information on writing, see the *Guide to Managerial Communication: Effective Business Writing and Speaking*, cited on page 111.

5. Email etiquette

In addition to the lessons you've learned in the previous section for traditional writing, keep in mind the common courtesies of "netiquette."

Composing email:

- Remember that business email etiquette differs from informal email with friends. Business email may involve more traditional use of capitalization and spelling.

- Visualize your reader. Because email is so commonplace in business, people tend to be too casual in this channel. You can be less formal when using it for business purposes, but don't be inappropriately casual. Because the recipient can't hear or see you, remember that there is room for misunderstanding on the receiver's end.

- Use a "talking" subject line that tells the reader what the message is about and how it concerns your reader.

- Pay attention to the first screen of your message. Make sure it includes any requests for action and previews the main points that follow.

- Edit into short chunks. Avoid huge blocks of text.

- Add headings, lists, or numbers that will make your email easier to skim.

- Use jokes, slang, and emoticons with care. Emoticons such as ☺ may harm your credibility with some readers. Use good judgment here. If you write to someone frequently and you have a less formal relationship, then emoticons are okay. However, if you're writing to a prospective employer or client, use words only.

Processing email:

- Check your email regularly and answer promptly, but resist the temptation to look at email or surf the web continually.

- Choose your recipients carefully. Avoid sending "reply to all" unless all recipients need to receive the message.

- Respond cautiously or delay responding. Don't send the email if you feel highly emotional or if you wouldn't be comfortable with your colleagues, your boss, or a reporter reading it. Avoid miscommunication caused by responding too fast and without reflection; email can leave a paper trail that may come back to haunt you.

For more on email etiquette, see the Munter, Rogers, and Rymer article cited on page 111.

6. Web page etiquette

Perhaps the most impersonal form of business communication, the web page, deserves some special etiquette attention. A web page can serve as a powerful business communication tool, but it can also be a source of frustration for viewers and can create a negative image of you.

Web page etiquette, like every other area of communication etiquette, requires paying attention to details and considering the needs of your intended audience. When designing a web page, keep these basic pointers in mind:

- Remember your audience. Everyone who has access to the Internet can view your web page. Don't be cute or place anything on your web page that could be misinterpreted or appear to be insensitive to others.

- Keep it simple. Avoid large screens, big graphics, and busy backgrounds. Make your main points on the first screen. Use short words, sentences, and paragraphs. Divide and summarize the text with subheadings.

- Respect slow modems. If you are a designer, you are probably an active surfer. Not everyone will have your expertise or access to technology.

- Make navigation easy. Clearly identify links for ease of navigation. Offer options and provide several links so readers can take control of where they are going during their visit to your web site. It's okay to place links on your web page, but send a note to the individual or web master as a matter of courtesy.

- Revise regularly. Check your site regularly, especially links, as they often move or are no longer functional.

- Include an email link. Make it easy for viewers to contact you by including an easily recognizable email link.

- Review and revise before posting. Do not post a site that is under construction. As you would with any professional communication, proofread before you post. Better yet, have several people proofread and evaluate for communication clarity, usability, effectiveness, and efficiency.

For more information on web page communication, see the Lynch and Horton book cited on page 111.

7. Public speaking etiquette

If the thought of public speaking gives you the jitters or makes you break out in a cold sweat, you aren't alone. One of the most commonly-reported fears of business people is public speaking. You may never get rid of the butterflies in your stomach when it is your turn to speak, but following some basic etiquette rules for the setting will help. There is no magic to speech writing or delivery—just hard work and practice.

Practice: Perhaps the most important piece of advice for public speaking is to practice. Before you step on stage, rehearse, rehearse, rehearse. Practice in front of a mirror. Note your eye contact, body language, and voice tone and modulation. Keep track of how long you have actually spoken. If possible, videotape or record a practice session. Ask a friend or colleague to listen to your speech and critique it. Ask for their advice on how you may improve your speech. By following these suggestions, you can get your message across to your audience and make a good impression.

Speeches: Unlike one–to–one or small group interactions, public speaking requires a different set of etiquette skills. Follow these basic rules and you will be well on your way to getting your message across to your audience while making a good impression.

Preparing:

- If you are asked to speak, your message is the focal point of the speech. Remember that your message—not you—is the reason for your invitation.

- Find out all you can about the group to whom you will be speaking. This will give you some ideas as to what they need or want to know, and how long you will be speaking.

- Limit your message to a few key points. After all, that is all your audience will remember.

- Test all audio-visual equipment before you speak. Be prepared with a backup plan in case the equipment fails. Always use the microphone if one is provided; only amateurs think it's not needed. Adjust it to your height before you begin speaking. If no microphone is available, be sure to project your voice to the rear of the room.
- Meet the person who will be introducing you before the event starts. Mail a copy of your biographical sketch or some introductory comments for your introducer's convenience. Bring a copy with you just in case the original copy has been lost.

Delivery:

- Don't stand up until your introduction is complete. Then, stay standing for your speech.
- Begin by welcoming the audience to the event or thanking them for the opportunity to speak. Recognize any dignitaries who may be present.
- Keep a copy of your speech in front of you. Admittedly, it's a crutch, but an important one if stage fright causes you to forget what you were planning to say.
- Don't lean on the podium or hold on to it. If you are nervous, your white-knuckled death grip will distract the audience. Take keys and coins out of your pockets before speaking to avoid those nervous jingles.
- Don't overdo humor. If you aren't a natural comedian, you will bomb. Make sure that any jokes you do use are appropriate for the audience.
- Keep a glass of water at the podium; it will come in handy if you develop a cough.
- Keep an eye on the time. Never, ever go over your allotted time, even if you have not completed your speech.

Question-and-answer sessions: Sometimes a question-and-answer period is scheduled after a speech. There are rules of etiquette for this as well.

- Remain standing at the podium if this is the case.
- When a question is asked, repeat it for the benefit of the audience, and don't say anything judgmental such as "That's a good question."

- Toward the end of the question-and-answer period, say something like "We have time for a couple more questions," to indicate that the period is coming to a close.

When mixing and mingling after your speech, continue to keep it simple. If congratulated, say "Thank you" or "I'm glad you enjoyed it." If challenged, don't try to justify your remarks or position. Simply say, "Thank you for your comments," or "That's an interesting thought/position."

For more information on public speaking etiquette, see the *Guide to Presentations* cited on page 111.

CHAPTER 5 OUTLINE

1. Basic dining behavior
   Focus on the purpose
   Think about timing
   Make everyone comfortable
   Avoid lengthy interruptions by others
   Drink alcohol cautiously
   Take accidents in stride

2. Basic table settings
   Food to the left
   Drinks to the right
   Utensils from the outside in
   Napkin

3. Basic table manners
   Chewing and cutting
   Using your hands and arms
   Eating the food
   Passing and serving
   Handling challenging foods
   Resting or finishing
   Serving and removing

4. Host etiquette
   Plan in advance
   Get things started
   End the meal

5. Guest etiquette
   Getting started
   Ordering
   Conversing
   Thanking

CHAPTER 5

Basic Business Dining Etiquette

Your boss invited you to lunch at an upscale restaurant to meet with a prospective client because of your technical expertise. This is your first "expense account lunch." What happens now? As either host or guest, your actions are always observed and poor manners can put you at a severe disadvantage. Proper etiquette can make or break a deal when you are dining out for business purposes.

It doesn't matter whether business meals are part of your normal routine or a new activity. What matters is knowing how to handle yourself professionally when food is mixed with business. Everything from job interviews and sales presentations to networking and contract discussions is fair game for a business meal. In this chapter, we'll look at the basics of dining etiquette—things you need to know in any type of setting. With a little bit of knowledge and practice, you can learn how to navigate any dining situation, as host or a guest, with confidence.

1. Basic dining behavior

In today's hurried world of fast food and eating on the run—or even at your desk—it is not uncommon to be unfamiliar with basic dining etiquette practices. In this section, we'll discuss the things you should consider before you go out to eat in a business setting.

Focus on the purpose.   Before you get too hung up on rules, think about the reason why you are having a business meal. No matter where or when you eat, you are always on stage and your manners are on display. If you are eating with others for business purposes, the snack bar, cafeteria, or restaurant becomes an extension of your office. Enjoy the food and company, but always stay focused on the fact that you are doing business.

Think about timing.   Business meals can happen at any time of the day or night. The time of day and place where business meals are scheduled and served sends an important message about the purpose. The longer the meal, the more time is dedicated to socializing during these meals.

- *Breakfast meetings* are becoming more common as busy business people try to schedule more activities into each day. It's okay to schedule early morning meetings, so don't be surprised by an invitation to meet at 7:00 a.m. (or even earlier). This early morning meal is usually simple, so it doesn't take long to eat; therefore, these early morning meetings usually last no more than an hour and a half. If you are not an early riser, set your alarm clock to get up a little earlier than usual. Arriving for a breakfast meeting looking like you just stepped out of the shower sends the wrong message.
- *Lunch meetings* are still the most common business meal. They may start any time after 11:30 a.m. and may last for up to two and a half hours.
- *Dinner meetings* are not time constrained. They take place after normal working hours and may extend for several hours. With relaxed time constraints, socializing may take a more significant role.
- *Business banquets* can take place at breakfast, lunch, or dinner—each with preset menus and tables planned and served for speed and efficiencies. These meals can range from somewhat formal to very formal, and often feature presentations following the meal. See page 80 for more details on banquets.

Make everyone comfortable.   Although the purpose of the meal is business, socializing still occurs.

- Meals begin with meeting or greeting those with whom you are eating (described on pages 20–26).

- After the introductions and greetings, it is time to begin or continue conversations (described on pages 23–24).

- If you are right handed, you will more naturally tend to speak to the person on your right; therefore, make it a habit to always speak first to the person on your left. This simple practice will ensure that you include everyone at the table in your conversations.

- If you find yourself at a smaller table, always make eye contact with everyone at the table when you are speaking, even when you are answering a specific question.

Avoid lengthy interruptions by others.   One of the biggest distractions you may encounter is running into other people you know. If you run into friends or acquaintances, be polite and say a quick hello, but don't engage in a lengthy conversation. Think before you introduce: bringing others into the conversation can distract from the reason behind why you have decided to eat together.

Drink alcohol cautiously.   Unless you are very familiar with your table guests, it is best to stick with nonalcoholic beverages when the dining setting involves business. This is especially true during the lunch hour. The "three-martini lunch" may have existed in the past but now it is just folklore and far from normal practice in today's business setting.

- If you do order an alcoholic drink, have only one and don't experiment with something new.

- If you are a guest, don't order an alcoholic beverage unless offered by your host.

- If you are the host, always ask if it is okay with your guest(s) before ordering. (See page 67 for more details on ordering and handling wine.)

Take accidents in stride.   If you spill something, don't overreact; everyone has accidents. Try to keep the spill from getting on anyone else. However, if it does so, apologize, offer to pay their cleaning bills, and continue with your meal and meeting.

2. Basic table settings

Before sitting down to a meal, take a look at how the table has been set. The figure below shows the items in a typical place setting for a four-course meal. Remember three simple rules: food to the left, drinks to the right, and utensils from the outside in.

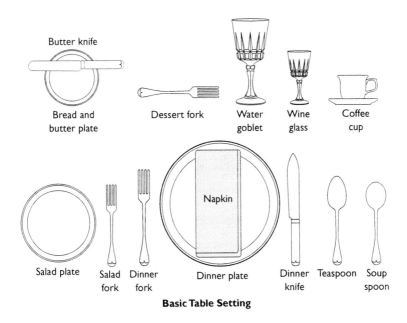

Butter knife

Bread and butter plate

Dessert fork

Water goblet

Wine glass

Coffee cup

Salad plate

Salad fork

Dinner fork

Napkin

Dinner plate

Dinner knife

Teaspoon

Soup spoon

Basic Table Setting

Food to the left:

- Your bread plate is either to the left of your forks or slightly above them.
- If a salad or fruit plate is part of the place setting, it will also be to the left of your plate.

Drinks to the right:

- Your water glass is to the right and above your knife and spoon.
- Your wine glass or glasses will be to the right of your water glass.
- Your coffee cup is also to the right.

Utensils from the outside in: The amount of silverware will depend on the formality of the meal. Remember to start with the outside piece and work your way toward your plate with each course.

- The salad fork is the farthest to the left of the plate if salad is served first.
- The dinner fork is closer to the plate.
- A dessert fork may be either closest to the plate or above the plate.
- The soup spoon is the farthest to the right of the plate because it is used first.
- The teaspoon is next, closer to the plate.
- The butter knife may be placed on the butter plate or between the teaspoon and the dinner knife.
- The dinner knife is next to the plate, cutting edge inward.
- If dessert is to be eaten with a dessert spoon, it will be placed above your plate.

Napkin: The napkin that you will use may be placed either to the left of your forks, on your plate, or in your water glass.

- After you sit down, pick up your napkin, unfold it, and place it on your lap.
- Never use your napkin as a handkerchief.
- Frequently dab your mouth with your napkin to remove any crumbs.
- If you need to leave the table, excuse yourself and place your napkin on the seat of your chair. It signals the service staff that you will be returning.
- When everyone is finished eating, fold your napkin and place it on the table beside your plate (never over your plate), but don't do this until everyone has finished eating—including dessert if served.

3. Basic table manners

Even if you were never taught basic dining matters, that is no excuse. Manners count—and successful business people know that they will be judged by their actions. As a quick refresher, here are some standard rules of etiquette that you may have learned at a very young age:

Chewing and cutting:

- Keep your mouth closed when chewing.
- Do not talk when you have food in your mouth.
- Always cut food into small pieces so that you can chew them quickly. You may need to respond to a question and should not have to chew for several minutes before you can answer.
- Never cut your entire entrée into pieces at one time. Cut off one or two small pieces at a time.
- Lean forward slightly each time you take a piece of food from your plate so that, if it should drop from your fork, it will fall onto your plate.
- In a perfectly proper setting, do not push food onto your fork with your knife or a piece of bread.

Using your hands and arms:

- Do not gesture when you have silverware or food in your hands.
- Keep your elbows off the table.
- Feel free to pick up foods that are almost always eaten with the fingers, such as crisp bacon, but it's always safe to cut up the food and use your fork. When in doubt, watch your host.
- If you find an olive pit, watermelon seed, piece of gristle, or something in your mouth that is distasteful, spit it discretely into a fork or spoon held close to your mouth.

Eating the food:

- Leave your plate as the server places it; do not rotate it.
- Never season your food before tasting it.
- It is okay to share foods, but never liquids. Do not pass your plate to have a shared item placed on it. Use a bread and butter plate or ask your server for a small plate.

- Once you have used a utensil, never let it touch the table again.
- If there is a problem with the food you have been served, get your server's attention and explain the problem in a soft voice.

Passing and serving:

- Generally, you should pass to the right.
- If someone requests an item, you would pass it directly to that person. Don't "shortstop" (that is, use something first); pass it directly to the person who made the request.
- If someone asks you to pass the salt, pass the pepper with it.
- Never reach across anyone to pass or to get an item. If you can't easily reach an item, quietly ask for it to be passed.

Handling challenging foods: Each of the following foods presents a unique challenge. Knowing how to handle them will increase your self-confidence and set you apart from the crowd.

- *Artichokes:* Using your fingers, remove the outer leaves one at a time and dip them in the dressing provided. Place the leaf between your teeth, with the soft side up, and scrape the fleshy part off by biting as you pull the leaf between your teeth. Then discard the leaf on the side of your plate. Do not eat the small leaves with sharp points or the prickly section near the bottom; remove and place them on the side of your plate. Using your fork, cut the center section (the "heart"), then dip each cut section into the dressing before eating it.
- *Asparagus:* You may eat asparagus with your fingers if the spears are firm and especially if there is a sauce for dipping. However, you will always be correct if you choose to use your knife and fork.
- *Bacon:* If the strips are crisp, you can use your fingers to eat it. If not, use your fork.
- *Cherry tomatoes:* These can be uncontrolled projectiles if placed in the mouth whole. Either cut or pierce them with a fork before eating.
- *French fries:* You may eat these with your fingers, but it is usually a good idea to use your fork.
- *Lemons:* Stick the tines of your fork into the pulp side of the lemon to avoid squirting the juice on you and those around you.

- *Parsley:*   Although usually a garnish, parsley is edible and serves as a natural breath freshener. Pick it up with your fingers and enjoy.

- *Pizza:*   Although tempting to use your fingers, pizza slices should be eaten with a knife and fork—except in the most casual of settings.

- *Shish kabob:*   Use your fork to push or pull the food items off the skewer. Eat with your knife and fork.

- *Tacos:*   They will be messy! Pick one up with your hands and hold it over your plate so that items will fall on the plate and not in your lap. Use your fork to eat what falls on your plate.

These are just a few of the foods that need special handling. If in doubt when faced with unique offerings, wait until your host or hostess begins to eat and follow his or her lead.

Resting or finishing: What you do with your utensils during a meal sends a message to your server. Placing your knife and fork in the position shown below indicates that you are still eating, but taking a pause.

Utensils in Rest Position

On the other hand, placing your knife and fork in the "4 o'clock" position, shown on the next page, indicates that you have finished your meal and your place setting may be removed. (And, as a final note to women: When you've finished eating, never, ever apply make-up at the table in a business setting.)

Utensils in Finished Position

Serving and removing: There is also specific etiquette for serving food and removing used items. Food should be served from your left side, with the left hand, and used items should be removed from the right side, with the right hand. (It is easy to remember this pattern if you think about how we read, left to right.) Beverages, on the other hand, are always served from the right.

So what happens if the service staff makes a serving mistake or if someone at your table errs when passing an item? Just let it go; it is never in good taste to mention it.

4. Host etiquette

In addition to knowing basic table manners, you should be aware of additional responsibilities and rules for hosting an event graciously. Here are some tips for planning in advance, getting things started, and ending the meal.

Plan in advance.

- *Focus on your purpose:*   You should have a clear idea of what you wish to accomplish at this meal. If you have more than one purpose, stay focused on your most important goals. Write each one down in the order they need to be achieved before you invite your guests. This simple activity clarifies not only the reason(s) for the meal, but also who should be invited.

- *Extend the invitation:*   Start your planning far enough in advance so that you can extend your invitation at least two weeks before the meal and your guests can plan their schedules. Be clear about where you will meet and how long the meeting should last. Furnish the name of the restaurant and its address and phone number. Make the reservation in both your name and your company's name.

- *Choose the venue:*   When you are hosting a meal, it is not a good time to experiment. Go to a restaurant with which you are familiar—one that has good food, excellent and timely service, and an atmosphere and table arrangements conducive to conversation. It is best to go to establishments where you are known; if you go often and tip well, the staff is more likely to know you and take excellent care of you and your guests.

- *Pay particular attention to seating arrangements:*   Place people in positions that help with the flow of conversation. Putting two introverts, who have nothing in common, next to each other can make for awkward silences.

- *Make arrangements in advance to pay the bill:*   Provide a credit card for imprint when you arrive and sign when you leave. This will avoid awkward moments when the bill is presented.

- *Cancel respectfully:*   If you have to cancel the event, always personally call those who you had invited. You don't need to give a reason for canceling, but make it a personal call. Never delegate this task unless it is absolutely necessary; a personal phone call sends the message that your guest(s) are very important to you.

Get things started.

- *Arrive early:* Arrive at least ten to fifteen minutes before the appointed time. Stay in the front waiting area of the restaurant so you can greet your guests. If there is no waiting area and you go to your table, do not touch anything on the table until your guests arrive. Turn off your pager and/or your cell phone when your guests arrive. However, keep them on until they arrive so you will be easy to contact if necessary.

- *Make menu suggestions:* Being familiar with a restaurant also provides you with a good conversation starter—menu suggestions. You can make recommendations to indicate items you especially like or to give your guests some clues about acceptable price ranges for their orders. Making a recommendation or an offer once is polite; making it a second time is pushy. Be careful of how much you are spending. You don't want to be considered cheap, but you don't want to be considered a show-off or spendthrift either.

- *Let guests order first:* As a good host, make sure that your guests' orders are taken first. Be sure to order the same number of courses as your guests to prevent awkward moments where you are eating and your guests are not. One exception should be noted here. You may want to suggest sharing a particularly interesting appetizer or dessert. Just ask your server to bring some extra plates so everyone can enjoy the item.

- *Order wine (if appropriate):* As the host, you set the stage.
  1. If you order alcoholic beverages, others will feel free to follow suit. Otherwise it sends a signal for others to abstain.
  2. When ordering wine for the table, wait until everyone has ordered entrées so that you can make the appropriate selection. With wine, as with menu items, it is best to stay in the mid-price range.
  3. When wine is presented, feel the cork for moistness and taste the wine. However, unless you are a true oeniphile (wine expert), do not sniff the cork! Ordering and accepting wine is different in business than is shown on television shows. Don't make a fool of yourself by pretending to know more than you do.

- *Start gracefully:* Unless the business is urgent, don't begin to discuss it until the end of the meal. Start by discussing everyday topics such as the weather, sports, travel, or other topics such as the décor of the restaurant. These opening gambits should lead to an easy, free-flowing conversational exchange. Engage in small talk before any business is conducted. A meal is really a social event until the order is taken.

- *Pace yourself:* During the meal, be considerate of your guest(s). Pace yourself by eating neither too quickly nor too slowly. If you are talking too much or asking too many questions, it will become obvious as you or your guest(s) haven't had a chance to eat. Unless you have agreed to discuss business ahead of time or are pressed for time, do not place business papers on the table until the meal is complete. However, you may leave business cards on the table to help you remember names when there are several new faces.

End the meal.

- *Ask your guests if they would like dessert.* Even if you are not interested, e.g., you might say, "The Death by Chocolate here is one of my favorites." Remember, this may be one of those occasions when you can suggest sharing. Check to see if they would like coffee or tea. Again, just as a guest will follow your lead, you should also follow their lead to make them feel comfortable. If they order dessert, coffee, or tea, follow suit. If you really don't want dessert, just order a cup of coffee or tea.

- *Lead the discussion.* After the meal, discuss business, make decisions, and conclude contracts as appropriate, placing only necessary papers on the table. Then, review what has been discussed, sum up actions still to be taken, and make sure everyone agrees with your summary.

- *Close the meal.* Place your napkin to the left of your plate and stand up. Accompany your guests to the door, shake hands, and thank them for joining you. By these simple actions, you send a clear signal that the meal and business has come to a close.

- *Motion to or ask your server for the bill.* Reach for the check immediately. Pull out your credit card or cash and make it clear that you are paying for the entire bill. Women should place their money or credit card somewhere in their purses where they can reach it quickly and easily. Don't place the check where your guest(s) can see the amount.

- *Tip appropriately.* TIPS is an acronym for *to insure prompt service,* so leave the right amount. These are only guidelines, so trust your judgment if you think you should depart from the following suggestions.
  1. 5 percent for the captain/maitre d' in a fine dining restaurant
  2. 10 percent for beverage service (15% for a sommelier—a special wine waiter in extremely formal restaurants)
  3. 10 percent for buffet service
  4. 15 percent for table service
  5. 20 percent for exceptional service or parties of six or more people
  6. $5 for valet parkers and $1 per coat for coat checkers

5. Guest etiquette

There are other specific rules for being a courteous guest.

Getting started:

- Confirm the date and time with your host a day or two in advance.
- Arrive on time or, better yet, a few minutes early. If you are delayed, contact your host to let him or her know you are running late and estimate your arrival time. Either call the restaurant to have a message relayed to your host or call your host's cell phone number
- Wait patiently in the waiting area if you arrive before your host. Do not sit in the bar or at your table and have an alcoholic drink—not even a beer or a glass of wine!

Ordering:

- Do not order either the least or most expensive item.
- Choose foods that are easy to eat as you carry on conversations. With that in mind, stay away from foods such as hamburgers, tacos, spare ribs, fried chicken, and spaghetti. Avoid finger foods. You never know when you might need to shake hands or handle some papers.
- Order an alcoholic drink only if your host does.

Conversing:

- Keep the conversation light and save the discussion of business topics until the end of the meal. Follow your host's lead in topics of conversation.
- Keep all unnecessary papers and materials off the table while you are eating.

Thanking: Always send a thank-you note.

- Send thank-you notes within two days of the occasion.
- Handwrite them on high-quality stationary, mentioning something specific about the occasion.
- Usually avoid a telephone call, fax, or email; they may appear too informal.
- Keep the message in your note simple; lengthy or elaborate notes are not necessary. For example: "Thank you for meeting me for lunch last Wednesday. Your insights were very helpful and will aid me in future plans."

The next chapter covers etiquette rules at more formal meals.

CHAPTER 6 OUTLINE

1. Invitations
   Issuing invitations
   Responding to invitations

2. Formal dining
   Service plate
   Appetizer
   Bread
   Soup
   Fish
   Sorbet
   Main entrée
   Salad
   Cheese and fruit
   Dessert
   Coffee and tea

3. Business banquets
   Checking out room arrangements
   Seating and starting

4. Casual dining
   In-house dining
   Picnics and barbecues
   Buffets
   Celebrations

CHAPTER 6

Special Dining Events

The doors swing open on a dazzling setting. It could be a movie set, but this ballroom scene is a formal business banquet and you are there! There are dozens of tables replete with centerpieces, water goblets, wine glasses, and, so it seems, countless knives, forks, and spoons. There are even place cards and menu cards. With more than a little bit of trepidation, you find your place card on a table. Now what do you do? Which one of the bread-and-butter plates is yours? Which fork or spoon should you use first?

The questions are swirling, but don't panic. You learned the basics for handling many of these questions in previous chapters. Whether you find yourself sampling *hors d'oeuvres* from a silver serving tray, being seated at a seven-course meal, digging in at a company barbecue, or sharing snacks at a retirement party, you can feel comfortable and participate with confidence.

I. Invitations

At some point, you will need to either send or respond to an invitation.

Issuing invitations: In the fast-paced environment of most business activities, invitations are usually extended through phone calls or emails. However, formal meetings, important celebrations, and important business meals require written invitations. The elements of all invitations remain the same.

- *The corporate/organization logo:*   It should be small and discrete, but clearly visible as an identifier.

- *The host(s):*   Identify the person who is extending the invitation, not just the organization.

- *The invitation:*   Phrases such as "invites you" or "your presence is requested" extend the invitation.

- *The type of celebration or event:*   Tell the recipient what to expect. It could be anything from brunch to cocktails and *hors d'oeuvres* to dinner.

- *The purpose:*   Let people know the purpose: for example, is it a grand opening, a retirement party, a product unveiling, an announcement, an introduction, or a year-end celebration?

- *The date:*   Name the day and date of the event.

- *The hour:*   Provide a specific starting time and provide an ending time if desired.

- *The place:*   Once again, be specific. Provide the restaurant's name, the street address, meeting room name or number, and any other identifiers that will help your guests find the location.

- *Special instructions:*   Helpful information about parking, dress, admission requirements, or other useful facts provides guidance for invitees and can help to avoid awkward moments.

- *Agenda or program:*   For formal banquets, ceremonies, and meetings, an agenda or program, along with a list of participants or invitees, will provide a context for activities. This courtesy allows everyone to prepare for the event and increase productivity.

Although not every occasion requires the degree of formality just listed, making a mental note of and following the elements of an invitation will help you avoid oversights, even in a casual setting.

Responding to invitations: Formal invitations will include an *RSVP* notation (*responde s'il vous plaît*), which means "respond if you please." In practice, this notation means you are obligated to respond. A contact person to whom you can convey your acceptance or regrets will be provided. Some invitations include reply cards for you to return. You should always respond to an *RSVP* within two days, even if only to give regrets. Some invitations have a "regrets only" notation. This means there is no need to respond unless you will not be attending the event.

2. Formal dining

On page 60, we discussed the basic table setting, which still holds true for formal dining—except that in formal situations, more courses are added. Each course has its own plate, glassware, and utensils. The illustration below shows a typical place setting that you would find for a very formal meal function.

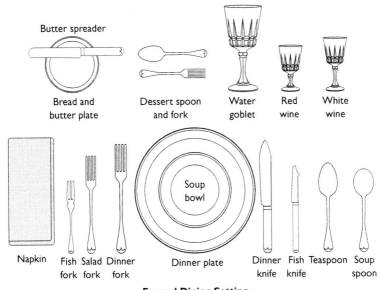

Formal Dining Setting

Although many possible courses are listed below, at most formal dinner functions today, the appetizer or the fish courses may be omitted and one or more courses combined (e.g., salad with the entrée, or dessert with coffee). Combining or eliminating courses not only speeds up service, but also simplifies the table setting. Common courses you might encounter could include the following:

Service plate: The service plate is also known as a "show plate" or a "charger."

- *What it is:* A special plate placed on the table before guests arrive. It is used to protect the table as well as to add decoration to the place setting.
- *Place setting:* If used, it will be in the middle of your place setting before the meal begins.
- *How it's used:* The plate is under the first course and is removed when that course is cleared.

Appetizer: These are called *"hors d'oeuvres"* in France, and "starters" in England.

- *What it is:* Various seafoods, fresh fruits, and other assorted, bite-sized pieces of food to whet the appetite. They may be accompanied by cocktails.
- *Place setting:* Waiters may serve appetizers while you are standing. If served while seated, the appetizer is brought out on a small plate, sometimes placed on your service plate.
- *How to eat:* (1) If appetizers are served while you are standing (either presented by a server or taken from a buffet table), take a napkin and leave it in your hand as long as you are eating appetizers. Never take food from the tray or buffet table and place it directly into your mouth; put it onto your plate or napkin before eating. There should be a container on the service tray or table to place food skewers or toothpicks after you've used them. If not, hold those items in your napkin until you find a wastebasket; do not place the used items back on the tray or buffet table. (2) If appetizers are served on an appetizer plate at the table, eat them with the small fork farthest to the left of the plate. If a platter is served, pass it to your right (counter-clockwise) around the table, always holding the platter so the person on your right can serve him- or herself.

Bread:

- *What it is:* Bread can be served as a whole loaf, a basket of sliced bread, or a basket of rolls. It is often served first or with the soup or salad course.
- *Place setting:* Your bread plate will be placed above and to the left of your dinner plate. (Remember: Food to the left and drinks to the right.) Your butter knife may be placed either across the upper edge of your bread plate or to the left of your teaspoon.

- *How to eat:*   (1) If the basket of bread or rolls is near you, take a roll or piece of bread and then pass the basket to the person sitting on your right (counter-clockwise). (2) If the basket is not near you, ask someone to pass it to you (likewise with the butter). (3) Place your bread selection onto your bread plate. (4) Always break off a bite-sized piece of roll or bread; never pick up the whole roll or slice of bread. (5) Use your butter knife or regular knife and butter that piece only. (6) Place your butter knife horizontally across the top of the bread plate, never back onto the table surface. (7) Put the entire but-tered piece into your mouth and chew with your mouth closed.

Soup:

- *What it is:*   The first course you might encounter at a business lunch or dinner could be soup. Soups can be hot or cold, clear or thick.

- *Place setting:*   Hot soups are usually served in a soup bowl and cold soups are usually served in soup cups, which may be accompanied by sherry. Your soup spoon is the largest spoon in the place setting and is lo-cated the farthest to the right of the plate.

- *How to eat:*   (1) Dip your spoon into the soup, skim away from you to-ward the opposite side of the bowl or cup, bring it to your lips, and sip it. (2) Don't blow on the soup to cool it and try not to slurp. (3) To finish your soup, tip the bowl away from you and dip your soup spoon into it. (4) Af-ter you have finished your soup, place your soup spoon on the saucer un-derneath the soup bowl. Never place your spoon in the soup bowl.

Fish:

- *What it is:*   A small portion of a mild fish sometimes served with a fleuron (small, crescent-shaped puff pastry garnish) that may be accom-panied with white wine.

- *Place setting:*   If this course is served, a fish fork and knife will be pro-vided. Both are smaller than the meat fork, and the knife will be the far-thest from the plate. The fish knife is also easy to recognize because the blade is shaped differently and, for bit of etiquette trivia, is made of silver because other metals react with the fish, increasing the "fishy" taste.

- *How to eat:*   When fish is served with the bone in, use the broad side of the knife to lift the fish carefully and separate a piece of fish, then use your fish fork to convey the fish to your mouth. If you are served a boneless fil-let of fish, just use your fish fork to cut the fish.

Sorbet:

- *What it is:*   A frozen pureed fruit or fruit juice, which may be flavored with a liqueur, offered to cleanse the palate before the entrée.

- *Place setting:*   The sorbet will be served in a small bowl or cup, on a small plate, with a small spoon.

- *How to eat:*   (1) Take a small amount on your spoon and eat it in several small bites. The portion may appear small, but it is not to be eaten in one bite. (2) After you have finished your sorbet, place your spoon on the saucer underneath the sorbet bowl. Never leave your spoon in the bowl or cup.

Main entrée:

- *What it is:*   Hot meats, vegetables, and often pastas, which may be accompanied with red or white wine.

- *Place setting:*   You will have a large dinner fork on the left and a large dinner knife on the right side of your plate. You may find a serrated steak knife at your place setting when red meat entrées are on the menu. The entrée itself will be served to you on a dinner plate.

- *How to eat:*   Generally, you will need to use your dinner knife to cut the meat and possibly some of the vegetables served with it. The American method is to: (1) Pick up your knife in your right hand and your fork in your left. Place your index finger just below where the handle meets the blade of the knife. (2) Use the fork to steady the item as you cut it. (3) Your elbow should be just a little above the table, not high in the air. (4) Cut one or two small pieces at a time. (5) Lay your knife across the top of your dinner plate, switch your fork to your right hand, and carry the food to your mouth. (The Continental method is to keep the fork in your left hand for both cutting and eating.)

Salad:

- *What it is:*   Salad greens (which may not all be green), edible flowers, meats, fruits, and/or nuts, which may be served with or without dressing.

- *Place setting:*   The salad fork is smaller than the dinner fork. It will be placed to the right of the dinner fork if the salad is served after the main entrée, to the left if served before the main entrée. Some settings also include a small salad knife. The salad fork and knife will be placed to the left and right, respectively, of your place setting.

- *How to eat:*   (1) The server will place your salad in front of you. (2) The salad dressing will either be on the salad or available in bowls or cruets on the table. In this case, when you are passed your choice of dressing, ladle a modest amount onto your salad, pass it to your right, or set it in the center of the table. (3) Eating salad can be tricky; sometimes ingredients are not cut into bite-size pieces. Therefore, be sure to cut any large pieces so that they will fit into your mouth easily. As with any food, cut one or two small pieces at a time. (4) Be particularly cautious with cherry tomatoes. They should be cut in half carefully (to avoid exploding juice) and eaten with your fork.

Cheese and fruit:

- *What it is:*   An assortment of different cheeses and fruits, typically passed on a serving platter.

- *Place setting:*   A small plate and fork should be provided just before the cheese and fruit are served.

- *How to eat:*   (1) A server will present a platter of cheese and fruit containing wedges and/or slices of cheese and fruit. (2) Large whole fruits should be quartered, cut into bite-sized pieces, and eaten with a knife and fork. Small fruits such as grapes and cherries can be eaten with your fingers. (3) When cheese is served as a wedge, always cut at an angle, preserving the wedge shape. (4) Start with milder cheeses and then move to stronger ones.

Dessert:

- *What it is:*   A sweet pudding, ice cream, mousse, cake, pie, or other pastry served at the end of a meal, which may be accompanied by champagne.

- *Place setting:*   Your dessert utensil—a fork or spoon depending on the particular dessert—will sometimes be brought when dessert is served or may be part of the original place setting. If so, it is sometimes placed closest to your plate alongside the rest of your silverware, or it might lie crosswise above your dinner plate area.

- *How to eat:*   (1) If the dessert is pudding, ice cream, or mousse, use a dessert spoon. If it is pastry or cake, use a dessert fork. However, if dessert is pie *à la mode,* you may use both. (2) When you have finished eating, place the dessert utensil on the dessert plate or saucer beneath, if there is one.

Coffee and tea:

- *What it is:* A hot beverage served at the end of the meal, either with dessert (American style) or after it (Continental style).

- *Place setting:* Like all beverage cups and glasses, your coffee cup is located to the right of your knives and spoons.

- *How to drink:* (1) After the server pours your coffee, customize it to your taste, stir it with the teaspoon (located to the right of your plate), and then place the spoon on the saucer, never in the cup or back on the table. (2) If you used a condiment that came in a packet, such as artificial sweetener or creamer, place the empty packet out of sight under the edge of your saucer. (3) If the server places a pot of coffee or tea on the table but doesn't pour, the person nearest the pot should pour for everyone, filling his or her cup last. (4) Do not take ice from your water glass to cool a hot beverage. (5) Do not dunk anything (such as doughnuts, cookies, or biscotti) in your coffee or tea.

For more information on formal dining etiquette, see Letitia Baldrige's *New Complete Guide to Executive Manners* or Emily Post's *The Etiquette Advantage in Business,* both cited in the Bibliography on pages 111–112.

3. Business banquets

Business events where food is served come in many forms, styles, and settings. One such event is a banquet—a simple or an elaborate, sometimes ceremonious, meal serving many people at one time.

Checking out room arrangements: Unlike traditional restaurant settings, business banquets are all a little different. Take a quick look at the room as you enter and pay attention to how it is set. Is the room arrangement formal or informal? Are there separate tables for socializing and dining? Is there a head table? Are there reserved tables? Is there assigned seating with place cards? Take note, because these are all cues to the formality or informality of the event. The more of these cues that are present, the more formal the event.

Seating and starting:

- If the setting is formal, with place cards, there may be a diagram or list near the entrance to help you find your seat.

- Once you locate your seat, remain standing until others arrive. This simple gesture of standing not only makes it more inviting for others to join you, but it also makes introductions easier. If you are standing, you don't have to stand up to shake hands or worry about reading name tags at a distance or reaching across the salad dressing and butter during introductions.

- Once one or two others have joined you, you may either sit down if it is awkward to remain standing or remain standing as a sign of respect if a dignitary or senior executive will join you.

- Regardless of who is at your table, do not begin eating until everyone has arrived. That preset salad may look tempting, but good manners require you to wait. The same holds true for the bread and rolls.

- Several items may be preset on the table before the meal. Once everyone is seated, if a preset item (such as salad dressing, bread, rolls, butter, and water) is located within easy reach, pick it up, use it, and then pass it to your right.

- If someone asks you to pass something that is out of his or her reach, simply pick it up and pass it without "shortstopping" (that is, using it yourself first).

4. Casual dining

The setting—a company cafeteria or lunch on the run—may seem casual, but that doesn't mean you don't need to observe the rules of dining etiquette. While you are enjoying your food or break from work, keep in mind that you are still being observed. How you handle yourself in these casual dining settings can affect your career!

In-house dining: Nowhere can distractions be more intrusive than when you dine in-house rather than going outside your work place for a business meal.

- Just because the setting is familiar doesn't mean that you can forget your manners. The same dining etiquette rules apply.

- When you invite someone to eat with you in on-premise food service facilities, put yourself in your guest's place: although the setting is familiar to you, everything could be new and possibly awkward to your guest. Therefore, when you arrive at the entrance, explain how food service is handled in your organization.

- Depending on common practices at your work place, others may join you at your table. So, be prepared to either introduce your guest or say that you are having a meeting with your guest and keep the interruptions to a minimum.

- When you are invited as a guest, the best bet is to follow your host's lead; the meal may be more of a social time than a results-oriented business meeting.

Picnics and barbecues: The foods served at these occasions bring on a whole new set of etiquette guidelines. You can forget about formal place settings and thinking about which fork to use first.

- Kick back a little! It's okay to eat fried chicken and barbecued ribs with your fingers and pile the dirty napkins in front of your plate.

- If you are asked to bring a dish to share, do so. If cooking is not your thing, stop by your favorite delicatessen or bakery to pick up something to share. However, be sure to remove the food from those cheap store containers and place it on a serving platter or in a bowl.

Buffets: The layout and quantities of food at a buffet may give you the impression of an "all you can eat" smorgasbord, but it is not.

• Practice moderation and don't overload your plate.

• Do not move a serving utensil from one dish to another. Use only the intended utensil for both sanitary and aesthetic reasons.

• Do not fill a plate and take it to your table for everyone to share. You should serve only yourself, not everyone seated at your table.

• Do not return for seconds until everyone has been through the serving line. At that point, it is acceptable to return, but use a clean plate when one is available.

• Although you serve yourself at a buffet, service personnel are often present to help with beverage service and the removal of dirty dishes. If they are not, notice where dirty dishes are being collected and clean up after yourself. It is not necessary, but it is polite to offer to take away someone else's dirty dishes when you remove your own.

Celebrations: There are a variety of reasons for business celebrations—promotions, retirements, transfers, milestone achievements, and recognition for a job well done—but the rules of behavior remain the same for all of them.

• There is always a purpose for a business social function, even if it's just called an office party, so make every effort to attend. Your conspicuous absence may be noticed if you do not attend. If your schedule prevents your attending, send an email or call your supervisor or the person in charge and let them know that you will not be able to attend.

• Greet the person in charge when you arrive.

• Keep celebrations in focus by recognizing the purpose and making the guest of honor the center of attention.

• Drink alcoholic beverages in moderation—if at all.

• Sample the *hors d'oeuvres*, but do not make a meal of them.

• Mix, mingle, socialize, practice your listening skills, and leave discussions about work-related topics to higher-ups.

- Let your superiors take the lead in introducing business topics.
- Thank the person in charge when you leave.

Special dining events are just that, special, so be attentive to the rules of etiquette for these occasions. Regardless of how often you go to any of these functions, it never hurts to review the basics before you attend.

CHAPTER 7 OUTLINE

1. Before the meeting
   Establishing a purpose
   Selecting participants
   Scheduling meetings
   Setting the agenda
   Arranging the seating

2. During and after the meeting
   Controlling the time
   Establishing ground rules before discussion starts
   Managing conflict
   Following up

3. Being a productive participant
   Before the meeting
   At the beginning of the meeting
   During the meeting

4. Distance meetings
   Teleconferencing (conference calls)
   Videoconferencing
   Electronic meetings

5. Parliamentary procedure

CHAPTER 7

Successful Meetings

"**W**hy do we always have our monthly meetings at 3 p.m. on the last Friday of the month? It seems like everything else is due on that Friday and sometimes all we do is listen to progress reports. Last Friday, we met for the full scheduled hour even though all the usual reports had been given in the first fifteen minutes. Oh well, I'll take some of my paperwork along, and if it gets too boring, at least I can be productive." Have you ever sat through meetings like this? Too many of us have, and these poorly-planned and poorly-moderated meetings have given a bad name to a critical need in organizations.

We can't solve all the problems with meetings in the next few pages, but the meeting etiquette information presented in this chapter will help you alleviate some of the common problems shared by many meeting-goers. With a little bit of planning and attention to proper meeting etiquette, these scheduled times together can be productive engagements for both organizers and participants.

1. Before the meeting

Bringing people together simply for the purpose of discussions can be a dangerous waste of everyone's time. You need to plan ahead to use the time wisely.

Establishing a purpose: Start by thinking about the purpose of a meeting. Is a meeting really necessary? Or would a memo, email, or web page posting accomplish the same purpose and be less disruptive to everyone's schedules? Are there decisions to be made? How many participants must be involved? Is there a need for information exchange and/or relationship building?

A clearly-defined purpose allows you to be considerate of other participants' time. If your planned meeting doesn't fall into one of the following need categories, think long and hard before succumbing to the meeting urge. In a meeting, you need to . . .

- Interact, because job activities are interrelated
- Establish, maintain, or revitalize relationships
- Exchange information
- Gain input from various sources
- Exchange ideas via brainstorming
- Identify and/or solve problems as a group, or
- Make group decisions

Selecting participants: Once you have identified the purpose for the meeting, ask yourself who should be involved. Consider how many people are necessary to achieve the purpose of the meeting, who will contribute to the purpose of the meeting, and who possesses the decision-making power to achieve the agenda. Invite only those participants who are needed for these purposes. You may want large numbers of participants when the meeting purpose is information sharing. However, remember that the larger the number, the more difficult the process will be to manage.

Scheduling meetings: Once you know your purpose and participants, schedule the meeting wisely. When selecting the best day and time, keep these guidelines in mind.

- Don't create meeting fatigue. Avoid the temptation to meet on set days and times just because it has always been done that way. Keep the number of meetings to a minimum, and everyone wins!

- Consider times and places that are agreeable and convenient for everyone.

- To avoid creating unnecessary stress, do not schedule meetings on the days before holidays or near the end of a business day.

Once the day and time have been set, observe these time savers and attendee considerations.

- For the convenience of attendees, and to aid in everyone's planning, send an email or distribute a memo that lists the time, date, and place well in advance.

- If the meeting is going to be a long one, provide breaks in the scheduled agenda so that participants can see to personal needs.

Setting the agenda: When preparing the agenda, remember that it creates a road map that directs the participants to a desired outcome and keeps the meeting focused and moving.

- Send a printed agenda to all attendees before the meeting. The most important items should come first in case you run out of time.

- Use the agenda to provide opportunities for participants to prepare for the meeting and provide meaningful contributions. Receiving the agenda before the meeting gives attendees time to research, discuss, and think about issues and topics before the meeting; to know what materials to bring with them; and to be prepared to discuss and provide input where appropriate.

- Bring extra agendas to the meeting in case anyone forgets his or her copy.

Arranging the seating: Before the meeting begins, consider the importance of seating arrangements. Table and chair arrangements can communicate the degree of formality and the kind of interaction you expect to take place.

- Place chairs, without tables, in a circle or horseshoe shape to encourage participation; straight lines of chairs signal a more formal meeting.

- Seat special guests and people in leadership roles near the moderator to focus discussions.

- Consider using a round table; that way, you never have to worry about who is seated at the head of the table.

- Separate people from different departments or units to encourage interaction and discussion between departments/units.

- In a formal meeting setting, place easily readable name cards with each person's title and organization (on both sides) on the table before convening.

- In less formal meetings, manage seating arrangements by placing an agenda or other materials at each place, with each individual's name written boldly across the top.

2. During and after the meeting

As the chair of a meeting, you are in charge—so take control and provide direction. The most productive meetings are those which deliver valuable information or generate frank, open, and creative discussions. As chair or moderator, you should foster such discussions, but ensure that the meeting remains focused on what you want to accomplish and information that needs to be shared. In addition, don't forget the importance of appointing someone to take accurate notes during the meeting. These minutes will ensure that important points of discussion, decisions, and action items are not forgotten.

Controlling the time:

- Begin and end on time. In most situations, start on time—every time— instead of waiting on late-comers. If attendees are unfamiliar with each other, begin by introducing everyone or having participants introduce themselves. Find out if anyone will need to leave early in case the agenda needs to be rearranged.

- Consider appointing someone to serve as scribe (note- or minute-taker) during the meeting. Don't be distracted by trying to moderate the meeting and write at the same time. A scribe can save time because everyone can focus on the discussion while the scribe can continue to record the key information.

- Once everyone is seated and/or introduced, begin by providing a brief overview of the meeting's purpose. When you are meeting in a strange place or have guests, ensure everyone's comfort. Let them know where the restrooms are located and when and if refreshments will be served.

- As you move through the agenda, create opportunities for open and honest discussion and avoid the tendency to dominate. You can encourage participation by (1) establishing ground rules for discussion; (2) interrupting monopolizers; (3) encouraging nonparticipants to contribute their thoughts and ideas; and (4) controlling conflict.

- End on time. If time is running short, handle only critical items and hold the rest of the items on the agenda until the next meeting.

Establishing ground rules before discussion starts: Discussions are an integral part of any meeting. Think about how much discussion will be beneficial and how you will control the flow. Remind participants that . . .

- Remarks should be relevant to the matter being discussed.

- Comments should be focused on ideas and issues, not people; disagreements are fine, but personal attacks are not acceptable.

- Everyone should be involved in discussions. It is your role as chair or moderator to ensure involvement. If someone has been silent, ask for his/her opinion.

Managing conflict: Conflict is inevitable and—in many cases productive—in the decision-making process. Don't be surprised when conflict occurs during meetings, but plan to manage it productively by . . .

- Letting each person state his or her points of disagreement completely.

- Keeping the discussion focused on issues and not personalities.

- Summarizing key points after everyone has had an opportunity to speak.

- If hostility continues, assigning the item to a smaller group charged with reviewing and reporting at the next meeting.

- Tabling the discussion to a later time or meeting (if conflict escalates to hostility); this will allow the combatants to cool off.

For more general guidelines and ideas on how to handle conflict, please refer to pages 32–33.

Following up: When the meeting concludes . . .

- Thank everyone for coming and give credit to those who have contributed or who deserve special recognition.

- If it has been a formal meeting that needs to be documented, have the minutes typed and distributed as soon as possible. Minutes should (1) summarize the key points of agreement and disagreement as well as actions taken, (2) provide a record for future reference, and (3) allow you to follow up on who should be doing what.

- If the meeting was informal, review your notes and identify needed actions.

- Review what worked and what didn't work at each meeting. Make note of your successes and learn from your failures.

3. Being a productive participant

Etiquette for meeting participation is just as important as etiquette for meeting management. If you are invited to attend a meeting, ask yourself why you have been asked to the meeting and prepare accordingly.

Before the meeting:

* Find out the reason for the meeting and your part in it.
* Review the agenda ahead of time and—unless you plan to add items to it at the beginning of the meeting—stick to it.
* Bring copies of the meeting materials with you. Don't expect copies to be handed out again at the meeting.
* Don't bring unrelated work to the meeting; you may be tempted to let your mind drift from the agenda.
* Be ready to listen and actively participate by both asking questions and providing input where appropriate.

At the beginning of the meeting:

* Be considerate and respect everyone's time by arriving early. Arriving late to a meeting is not only rude, but is also disrespectful to all of the participants.
* Introduce yourself to attendees you don't know.
* Don't walk in and take just any seat if you are joining a meeting for the first time. Wait for others to be seated, especially the moderator, and then find yourself a seat.
* Keep all you think you will need on the table in front of you, but place your briefcase or purse on the floor beside your chair.

During the meeting:

* Don't hesitate to speak, but make sure you have something to contribute and say it in as few words as possible. Avoid dogmatic statements. Make sure you speak loud enough to be heard.
* Don't interrupt anyone. Wait until there is a break in the discussion or you are called upon before speaking. Your comments won't be heard if others are talking.

- Don't engage in private conversations during the meeting. If your thoughts and comments are important, share them with everyone.

- Be mindful of your body language. Don't let any boredom, tiredness, or frustration show.

- Don't lean back in your chair and cross your arms. These postures may communicate defensiveness or a closed mind.

- Instead, stay focused on the purpose of the meeting. Sit up straight with both feet on the floor and maintain eye contact to look attentive and engaged.

4. Distance meetings

The power of personal, face-to-face interactions may never be replaced. However, the convenience and cost savings of electronically-mediated meetings has driven this meeting format to be used increasingly. Such meetings may take place with participants in the next office, different areas of the same building, or in different cities or countries via telephone, video, or email.

Teleconferencing (conference calls):

- Figure out how many participants can be accommodated on your phone systems. Larger numbers may require preparing a conference call identification code or may need operator assistance.

- Contact participants to determine each one's availability on specific dates and at specific times. Provide at least three alternate times and dates for meeting possibilities and be sure to specify which time zone will be used for the call. When mutually-agreeable times are not available, find the one that works best for the most important participants (rank or office) and ask others to rearrange their schedules.

- Distribute the agenda via email before the scheduled call.

- Reconfirm the date and time with all participants the day before the call.

- Clear your calendar before the call and log in a couple of minutes ahead of the scheduled time.

- Identify yourself. You should hear a tone once you have successfully logged in. Wait two or three seconds after you hear the tone to be sure you won't interrupt anyone. Then, offer a greeting followed by your first and last name—even when you know all of the other participants.

- When there are several participants, state your name before making a comment.

- Listen carefully. Speak only when necessary, but don't hesitate to speak; this is the only way people will know you are participating because you are not visible to the other participants.

Videoconferencing: The same rules of etiquette that hold true for teleconferencing also hold true for videoconferencing. However, in this format, everyone is on camera and on stage, so a bit of extra planning is needed.

Before the meeting begins:

- Work with a technician to ensure that all equipment works and that you know how it operates.
- Practice using all equipment as you will during the videoconference.
- Make sure that you have everything you need for the meeting on the desk or table in front of you. Remove anything that may distract the other participants before the videoconference begins.

During the meeting:

- Be yourself. Imagine that you are actually sitting in a room with others. Be comfortable and confident. Smile and maintain eye contact by looking into the camera.
- Limit your motions because the camera can exaggerate them. Even though videoconferencing technology continues to improve, movements can be transmitted as distracting jerks.
- Speak a little slower and louder than normal and speak distinctly, enunciating your words, because the audio portion can be slightly delayed.
- Dress in solids and pastels; stay away from plaids and patterns which don't work well on camera.
- Be careful of body language. You never know just when the camera will focus on you just as you are scratching your nose or making a face at a comment someone has just made.
- Avoid side conversations and annoying sounds like coughing near a microphone, tapping your fingers or pen, or shuffling papers.

Electronic meetings: A third option for distance meetings is through electronic meeting systems (EMS). EMS involves the use of groupware and a trained facilitator. These meetings are like instant messaging: participants "meet" using a keyboard and screen, usually from their own work station. Their comments appear, in real time, on all participants' screens simultaneously. They allow shy people to participate more, notes to be generated immediately, and the flexibility of participants being in different places. To participate in EMS . . .

- Follow the established protocol for logging on to a password-protected site. Once log-on has been completed, the "floor" is open for contributions and collaboration.

- Remember that you are in a business setting. All you have learned about meeting etiquette holds true, even as you sit "alone" at your computer keyboard.

- Make your input count. Although instant messaging is a powerful part of electronic meetings, it is not the same as talking with friends.

- Even though you may choose or be instructed to submit questions or comments anonymously, use this feature with caution. Don't submit anything to which you would not want your name attached.

- Beware that anonymity may also lead to too much honesty, which creates conflict.

5. Parliamentary procedure

When meetings grow in size, keeping order, controlling the flow of discussion, and reaching agreements can become a challenge. One way to ensure decorum at any type of meeting is to follow parliamentary procedure. As the name implies, these rules for conducting formal meetings grew out of the practices of the British Parliament. *Robert's Rules of Order* first appeared in 1876 and had been updated through the years to meet the needs of meeting participants worldwide.

Parliamentary procedure is designed to aid decision-making and provide accuracy, efficiency, impartiality, objectivity, and uniformity in meetings. It ensures that, in the end, the majority will prevail but that contributions from the minority will be heard. Using parliamentary procedure is standard in many formal meetings; not knowing its basics may put you at a disadvantage as some of the terminology may sound like a foreign language.

Even if you don't participate in formal meetings, don't be surprised to hear parliamentary procedure terms being used in any meeting setting. Usage of these formal terms has spilled over and become commonplace in all types of meeting. Knowing the meaning of common parliamentary procedure motions used in formal meetings will give you the confidence to conduct or participate in meetings whenever this type of language is used. Understanding the following terminology will help you follow the flow of meetings.

- *Quorum:* the number of members who must be in attendance to conduct business legally. This requirement is protection against unrepresentative actions being taken by a minority. It could be any number, but if not stated otherwise in your bylaws, the quorum is a majority of the members.

- *Being recognized:* having the floor. You cannot speak until you are recognized by the chair and given the floor.

- *Motion:* a statement to bring a certain matter to the attention of the group. You may discuss items only after a motion has been made and seconded. A "seconder" does not necessarily agree with the motion, but does believe that the subject should be brought before the meeting for discussion. This is the only topic that can be discussed at this time.

- *Amendments:* to delete or strike out, to add or insert, and to strike out and insert language in the original motion. There is no such thing as a "friendly" amendment. This type of motion is not permitted, because it would place control in the hands of two participants—the proposer of the amendment and the maker of the original motion. A simple majority ratifies most amendments.

- *Call the question:* to call for an end to debate. This motion needs a two-thirds vote to pass.

- *"Tabled" or "Postponed":* motions to postpone a decision (to allow time for additional thought, for the collection of additional information, or for emotions to cool off).

These are only a few of the terms that may be used in parliamentary procedure. For more details, consult *Robert's Rules of Order* or a meeting parliamentarian. For more information on meetings in general, see *Guide to Meetings*, cited on page 111.

CHAPTER 8 OUTLINE

1. Preparing for your trip

2. Greeting people
   Touching
   Business cards
   Nonverbal behaviors
   Formality issues
   Language issues

3. Establishing relationships
   Practice patience
   Avoid certain topics
   Recognize the importance of religion
   Talk about safe subjects
   Interpret gestures correctly
   Remember color connotations
   Translate "yes," "no," and silence
   Understand personal space
   Expect different attitudes about time

4. Eating and gift giving
   Eating, a universal practice with twists
   Customary and appropriate gift giving

5. Considering gender issues
   Dress conservatively
   If in doubt, decline social invitations
   Expect traditional courtesy gestures

CHAPTER 8

Cross-Cultural Etiquette

It's your first business trip! You've been inundated with information about customs, currencies, and courtesies. You've even been warned to be observant and do as others do because you will be dealing with people from other countries at your meetings. If you thought the rules of etiquette in the United States seemed a bit complex, you'll come to realize that they are simple compared to some of the intricacies you may encounter in international settings.

It would be delightful if you could categorize people by country and culture and know exactly what to do in each setting. However, today's globalization has led to such a blending of cultural customs and practices that exact rules are impossible to make. Even so, knowing something about the basic do's and don'ts of countries and cultures around the world will sensitize you to avoid major *faux pas*. This chapter won't make you an etiquette expert in every international setting, but it will provide you with helpful hints when you interact with customers, clients, or guests from other countries—either at home or abroad.

1. Preparing for your trip

Variations in cultures and customs can throw a variety of new twists into the business etiquette arena. International travel can be fun, but, no matter how experienced you are, it can still be a little stressful. It's all too easy to put your foot in your mouth unintentionally and possibly insult your international colleagues.

- *Become sensitive to differences.*   Become familiar with the other culture and truly care about and respect differences.

- *Research and read about your destination* before leaving home. Talk with someone who has lived in the country or consult a travel guide or culture source book. At the very least, learn the basic, visible behaviors such as greetings, rituals, manners, and nonverbal behaviors. If possible, try to learn about the "hidden values" of the culture. As communication expert Mary Munter points out, "A single party conversation on the topic of international issues will probably not be sufficient; the more you can learn about economics and industry, politics and government, religion and philosophy, history, symbols and traditions, social structures, cultural achievements, language, sports, and food, the more successful you will be."

- *When in doubt, ask.*   Before venturing into the etiquette vagaries of other cultures and countries, always follow one simple rule: when in doubt, ask. It is okay to admit you don't know everything about global etiquette, and, by asking, you demonstrate that you are interested in learning, sensitive to differences, and want to be respectful.

- *Be careful not to stereotype.*   Not all people from the same country or culture act the same, so be flexible and ready for the unusual and unexpected. Remember that learning cultural norms means you can expect most of the people to behave a certain way most of the time, not that all of the people will behave that way all of the time.

- *Enjoy the "international" part of business relationships* by recognizing the uniqueness of the setting. Successful business people recognize that their organizations are part of the global economy. Those who are ethnocentric, and cling to the parochial viewpoint that their culture's way of doing business is the best way, will eventually offend their international counterparts.

2. Greeting people

Once you have arrived, be prepared to follow the customs of the country you are visiting. The differences you encounter may be surprising.

Touching: Touching is a social activity, deeply rooted in cultural values. In Western culture, we take handshakes for granted. They are almost automatic in our business world, but not so in every culture. So, the question, "To shake or not to shake?" is a good one to ask yourself in any international setting. You may notice these differences in greeting styles when in . . .

- *Asian countries:*   Bowing is in order but don't make a show of it. It is a simple means of displaying respect while greeting. However, with the younger business generation, handshakes are quickly becoming the norm.

- *Mediterranean countries:*   Kissing on both cheeks rather than shaking hands may be appropriate at the first meeting.

- *Latin American countries:*   Don't be surprised if you are greeted with a strong embrace rather than a handshake. Long handshakes, hugs, and even grabbing the elbow or shoulder during a greeting may be appropriate here.

- *Middle Eastern countries:*   A handshake between men is in order, but prepare for it to be very limp. In these countries, the handshake may often resemble handholding rather than the firm and brief handshake to which you are accustomed.

Business cards: Business cards serve a variety of purposes, from communication devices to conversation starters. In international settings, they are vital for establishing and maintaining relationships. Therefore, . . .

- *Remember to exchange business cards* as a courtesy and a communications aid.

- *Have your business cards printed on two sides.* If you will be dealing with several people in a specific country, print one side in English and the other in the local language.

- *Present and receive business cards* with both hands in Asian countries. Be sure to have the side with the host country language face up.

- *Never use your left hand* to offer or receive a card (or anything else) in Middle Eastern or predominantly Muslim countries. To put it politely, the left hand is reserved for "unclean" functions in these cultures.

- *Take the time* to read the information provided on the card when it is offered to you. This simple act shows your interest in the person.

Nonverbal behaviors:

- *Smiles:*   Because a smile can be interpreted as being disrespectful or overly casual, avoid the jovial, glad-to-meet-you approach when meeting or greeting members of non-Western cultures for the first time.

- *Eye contact:*   Although most Americans believe eye contact shows openness, other cultures—especially Asian ones—may view this gesture as showing disrespect, or even hostility, during initial greetings.

Formality issues:

- *Names:*   In the United States, people tend to address people by their first names as soon as introductions are made. This is not true in most other countries and cultures, where formality is the norm. Wait to be asked to use first names, and don't be surprised if the invitation is never issued. In addition, make sure you are prepared to pronounce names correctly.

- *Titles:*   Address people with their formal titles. Learn what titles mean because they vary by country.

- *Rank and status:*   In international settings, rank and status may be particularly important. Pay attention to cues such as dress, office space and decorations, and position within the organization. Treat everyone as important, but recognize that those who have attained positions of importance expect to be treated as special.

Language issues: English may be the universal language of business, but always make an attempt to speak a few words of the local language first to show you are making a sincere effort to appreciate the other person's culture.

- At a minimum, learn some basic terms and phrases. Learn to greet, thank, apologize, and toast in the local language.

- Avoid speaking loudly, which will not help if someone doesn't speak your language.

- Use an interpreter if necessary. Help the interpreter by speaking slowly and enunciating. Stop after each couple of sentences to allow time for the translator to speak.

3. Establishing relationships

Once greetings and opening pleasantries have been exchanged, consider what it takes to establish lasting relationships. Think about issues such as timing, conversation topics, gestures, color choices, and personal space. Recognizing and practicing local customs will set the foundation for future success.

Practice patience. Americans often spend precious little time getting to know others before getting down to business. This "let's get down to business and avoid personal niceties" attitude and approach may work well in Anglo and Nordic cultures, but could lead to disaster in Asian, Latin American, and Middle Eastern countries, which value building relationships before conducting business.

Avoid certain topics.

- *Jokes:* Remember that what may be funny to you could be insulting in another setting.

- *Politics:* A discussion of politics may be okay at home, but just think about how passionate some people you know become when the topic of conversation turns to this subject. Your lack of understanding about the intricacies of other cultures and political issues could inadvertently lead to embarrassing or insulting comments.

- *Religion:* No matter what the international setting, whenever possible, avoid any discussion dealing with religious or other very personal topics.

Recognize the importance of religion. Although you should avoid discussing religious topics, remember that observance of religious norms can be very important in many international settings, especially in Islamic cultures.

- *Learn a few basics* about the predominant religion(s) of the regions you will be visiting.

- *Pay particular attention to time,* as well as days of the week, when business activities should be avoided. For example, there is a call to prayer five times a day and the Sabbath is celebrated on Friday in the Muslim world. In Israel, businesses may close at noon to begin preparations for the Sabbath, which is from sundown on Friday to sundown on Saturday in the Jewish world.

• *Note religious holidays.* Be aware of holidays (religious and otherwise) when business dealings must be avoided, such as Rosh Hashanah, feasts of patron saints, Ramadan, the Chinese New Year, and summer holidays. Countries that are predominately Roman Catholic celebrate high holy days such as The Epiphany of Christ, the Ascension of Christ, and All Saints' Day.

Talk about safe subjects. With all of these taboos, what can you talk about? As with any initial conversation, the weather, sports, architecture, natural wonders, or local culinary delights are always a good start. Other topics include knowledgeable references to the history, art, architecture, and unique geographic features of the country. Most people are justifiably proud of their country and heritage.

Interpret gestures correctly. Seemingly simple and innocent gestures that are everyday occurrences in many Western cultures can be offensive in other parts of the world. Body language doesn't always translate the way you intend, and can lead to unintended etiquette blunders. Think about some of these gestures that we often see and sometimes use.

• Gestures that you may be accustomed to using—like the "okay sign," "thumbs up," "V for victory," and beckoning with a crooked finger— could all be considered insulting, depending on the country.

• Pointing with the index finger and touching someone with the left hand would be considered impolite in Arab culture.

• Showing the soles of your shoes to anyone in many Buddhist and Islamic countries is considered an insult; therefore, avoid crossing your legs at the ankle because your guest will see the bottom of your shoe.

• Nodding your head up and down means "no" in Bulgaria.

• Pointing your chopsticks at someone or sticking them in your rice is considered an insult in many Asian cultures.

• Even a simple gesture like putting your hands on your hips could be considered rude or hostile in the wrong setting. For example, in Argentina, it would be considered a challenge.

Remember color connotations. Something as seemingly simple as your choice of colors in the clothes you wear, the gifts you give, the slides you use for a presentation, or the printing on your business card can send strong messages. Depending on the country or culture, these messages may be positive or negative. Here are just a few examples of how colors convey different meanings around the world.

- In the United States, the combination of red, white, and blue symbolizes patriotism, black indicates death and mourning, and red means danger and warning.
- In Asian countries, white is the color associated with death or mourning.
- In Islamic countries, green is considered a sacred color. You would have to be very careful in your use of it or you could inadvertently create a religious insult. However, in Ireland, green might be seen as patriotic.
- Never write the name of a living person in Korea in red. Yet, if someone in Great Britain wins a red ribbon, it is an honor symbolizing first place.

Translate "yes," "no," and silence. Think about the following two questions and base your answers on personal experiences. What does it mean to you when you hear the words "yes" or "no?" Would you be comfortable carrying on discussions with a foreign counterpart when you are suddenly faced with a long period of silence?

- Americans confer precise meanings to the words "yes" and "no." However, in many cultures—especially Asian ones—a "yes" can simply mean that the other party understands what you are saying, not that they agree with you. In these settings, don't expect to get "no" for an answer. Telling you "no" could be considered impolite. Even if there is disagreement, you won't detect it by hearing the word "no."
- Americans are often uncomfortable with even short moments of silence. Yet Asians, especially Chinese and Japanese, use long periods of silence to think before responding.

Understand personal space. Different cultures also attach varying acceptable limits for public and private space. If we define "intimate" space as that appropriate for comforting or greeting, personal space as that for talking with friends, social space as that for talking with strangers, and public space as that for standing in lobbies or reception areas, then keep the following in mind:

- Americans prefer zero to eighteen inches for intimacy, eighteen inches to four feet for personal space, four to twelve feet for social space, and more than twelve feet for public space.

- Countries with a Latin heritage usually prefer much closer personal and social space; therefore, they could consider it rude if you back away.
- The British may favor more distant personal and social space and could consider it rude if you stand too close.

Expect different attitudes about time.   What is an appropriate time frame for one culture may not be appropriate for another. Some cultures expect an exact and precise timetable; other cultures have a more relaxed attitude toward time.

- *Time is precise:*   In some cultures (such as the United States and Northern Europe), people are very sensitive to the value of time and regard attention to punctuality as a sign of professionalism and respect.

- *Time is relaxed:*   People in many other countries and cultures (such as South American and Mediterranean countries) view time differently. These cultures may have a more relaxed attitude about the significance of punctuality.

- *Time is not specific:*   A meeting that is scheduled for a set time may actually start much later, and it may even be inappropriate to arrive on time. Imposing deadlines and firmly sticking to time schedules in these cultural settings could be considered unprofessional and even rude.

- *Interruptions:*   In some cultures, interruptions may be accepted as a normal business practice and are not considered distractions or annoyances.

4. Eating and gift giving

Two special etiquette issues encountered in cross-cultural settings center on eating and gift giving. To ignore the importance of either may lead to etiquette disasters.

Eating, a universal practice with twists: Everyone needs food and everyone eats. The questions here are "when?" and "what?"

- *When people eat:*   People in the United States normally have breakfast between 6 a.m. and 8 a.m., lunch between 12 noon and 2 p.m., and dinner between 6 p.m. and 8 p.m. However, people in other countries can be different. The French cannot understand our insistence on breakfast meetings. To them, it is a leisurely beginning to the day with croissants, coffee, and the morning paper. In Spain and many Latin American countries, lunch can be eaten from 1 p.m. until 3 p.m. and dinner may not start until around 10 p.m. In many Asian countries, going out for alcoholic drinks after work may be an automatic extension of workday responsibilities.

- *What people discuss:*   In many countries, business dinners and social functions include extensive socializing and drinking before any business is conducted. Refusing to join in the festivities, or bringing up business subjects too soon in these settings, would be considered very rude. Business meals in some countries are business in name only. They are a time for socializing, so never bring up business subjects unless your host or hostess initiates the topic.

- *What people eat:*   In many countries, food may be a symbol of prestige, honor, and wealth. In Asian and Middle Eastern countries, you may be offered far more than you can comfortably eat. If you know you will be dining out, plan ahead and save a little room. If offered chicken feet in China, recognize that you are indeed a very special guest, held in the highest esteem. So, you might not want to ask what something is before eating it. Just ask your host how the dish should customarily be eaten.

Customary and appropriate gift giving: Always carry items that could be used as gifts.

- Find out in advance what would be considered appropriate in your host country and when the gift should be given and /or opened—such as the beginning or end of your visit or at dinner. Regardless of the country, your gift should be beautifully wrapped.

- Select gifts that will have meaning to the recipient. Meaningful gifts are more appropriate than extravagant ones.

- Don't try to outdo others by giving them something considerably more expensive than they may be able to give you.

- Remember that someone, either you or your visitor, will have to pack the gift to take home. Therefore, keep them small in size and nonbreakable whenever possible. If you do choose something large, offer to have it shipped.

The following list of possible gifts is not complete, but it should start you thinking about what could be appropriate and, more importantly, inappropriate. As you have already seen, the meaning of colors are deeply rooted in customs, so it always makes sense to ask if there are any taboos or hidden meanings before presenting gifts or awards.

- *Good choices:* (1) local handicrafts from your home country, (2) coffee table books, (3) edible items, especially if associated with your region or country, (4) company or organizational give-always such as pens, mugs, key chains, and paper weights, (5) personalized gifts, (6) items clearly identified with your home country or region, and (7) pen-and-pencil sets.

- *Bad choices:* (1) time pieces in Asian countries because they are considered inappropriate, (2) knives or anything with blades in Latin American countries because this is a sign of "cutting" a relationship, (3) a handkerchief in the Middle East (a symbol of tears and parting), (4) alcohol in Muslim cultures because the Koran prohibits alcohol, and (5) fragrances or clothing because they send too many mixed messages.

- *Flowers:* (1) Yellow flowers symbolize mourning to many Latinos and Middle Easterners; however, in Chile, they symbolize contempt. (2) In Western Europe, chrysanthemums of any color and white lilies are associated with cemeteries. (3) Just like in the United States, red roses may communicate romantic intentions in many countries, especially in France and Peru.

5. Considering gender issues

When it comes to gender equality, many parts of the world don't follow the same practices as those of westernized countries. Nowhere are cultural differences in etiquette more discernible than for women doing business in male-dominated societies. These differences can be pronounced and sometimes awkwardly obvious in predominantly Islamic countries of the Middle East, Asia, and Northern Africa. However, there are also subtle, if not as important, differences, in Latin American and Southern European countries. A few reminders and practices can go a long way toward avoiding awkward moments.

Dress conservatively and avoid doing anything that could be construed as flirtatious or provocative. Avoid excessive jewelry, provocative perfume, striking make-up, vivid nail polish, and hairstyles that are not conservative and professional.

- *In Islamic countries:* Women should dress so that elbows and knees are covered; high-collared tops are also in order.
- *In Buddhist countries:* Women should not wear sleeveless or short-sleeved tops and shorts.
- *In all countries:* Dress as a business professional and expect to be treated as such.

If in doubt, decline social invitations unless you know who else is being invited and the reasons for the invitation. Think about the appropriateness of settings that may convey mixed messages, such as parties, dinners, or other social settings that create impressions of intimacy. Don't accept invitations to be entertained alone at the home of foreign business associates, unless it is a family affair.

Expect traditional courtesy gestures. Men in some cultures may open doors and pull out chairs at meals for women. What may be considered "old fashioned" or "condescending" here in the United States may be considered good manners in another country or culture.

For more information on courtesy in other countries, read *Guide to Cross-Cultural Communication* by Sana Reynolds and Deborah Valentine, cited on page 112.

BIBLIOGRAPHY

Baldrige, Letitia. *Letitia Baldrige's New Complete Guide to Executive Manners.* New York: Rawson Associates, 1983.

Baney, Joann. *Guide to Interpersonal Communication.* Upper Saddle River, NJ: Prentice Hall, 2004.

Bixler, Susan and Nancy Nix-Rice. *The New Professional.* Holbrook, MA: Adams Media.

Code of ethics: Hospitality Service and Tourism Industry in *Ethics in hospitality management,* Stephen S. J. Hall, ed., Education Institute of the American Hotel and Motel Association, 1992.

DeTienne, Kristen Bell. *Guide to Electronic Communication.* Upper Saddle River, NJ: Prentice Hall, 2002.

Eichler, Lillian. *The Customs of Mankind.* Garden City, NY: Garden City Publishing Company, Inc., 1924.

Fox, Sue. *Business Etiquette for Dummies.* New York: Wiley Publishing, Inc., 2001.

http://www.echopsticks.org/chopsticks-history.html

Giblin, James Cross. *From Hand to Mouth.* New York: Harper Collins, 1987.

Goldsborough, Reid. "Words for the Wise: Writing for the Web," *Office Systems.* November 1999, 52.

Lynch, Patrick J. and Sarah Horton. *Web Style Guide.* 2nd ed. New Haven, CT: Yale University Press, 2002.

Mitchell, Mary and John Corr. *The Complete Idiot's Guide to Business Etiquette.* Indianapolis, IN: Alpha Books, 2000.

Munter, Mary. "Cross-Cultural Communication for Managers." *Business Horizon.* May–June 1993, 69–78.

Munter, Mary. *Guide to Managerial Communication.* 6th ed. Upper Saddle River, NJ: Prentice Hall, 2002.

Munter, Mary and Michael Netzley. *Guide to Meetings.* Upper Saddle River, NJ: Prentice Hall, 2002.

Munter, Mary, Priscilla S. Rogers, and Jone Rymer. "Business Email: Guidelines for Users." *Business Communication Quarterly.* March 2003, 26–40.

Munter, Mary and Lynn Russell. *Guide to Presentations.* Upper Saddle River, NJ: Prentice Hall, 2001.

Netzley, Michael and Craig Snow. *Guide to Report Writing.* Upper Saddle River, NJ: Prentice Hall, 2001.

Post, Peggy and Peter Post. *Emily Post's the Etiquette Advantage in Business.*
    New York: HarperCollins, Publishers, Inc., 1999.
Powers, Dennis. *The Office Romance: Playing With Fire Without Getting
    Burned.* New York: AMACOM, 1998.
Reynolds, Sana and Deborah Valentine. *Guide to Cross-Cultural
    Communication.* Upper Saddle River, NJ: Prentice Hall, 2004.
Robert, Henry M., III, William J. Evans, Daniel H. Honemann, and Thomas J.
    Balch. *Robert's Rules of Order, Newly Revised.* 10th Ed. Cambridge, MA:
    Perseus Publishing.
Smith, Huston. *The World's Religions.* New York: HarperCollins, 1999.
Yale, Laura. "Manners Matter." *Tourism: The Business of Travel.* 2nd ed. (by
    Roy A. Cook, Laura Yale, and Joseph Marqua), Upper Saddle River, NJ:
    Prentice Hall, 2002.

Index